German Mountain Troops
in World War II

German Mountain Troops

in

World War II

A Photographic Chronicle of the
Elite *Gebirgsjäger*

Roland Kaltenegger

Schiffer Military History
Atglen, PA

Translated from the German by David Johnston
Book Design by Ian Robertson.

Printed in China.
ISBN: 0-7643-2218-4

This book was originally printed under the title,
Gebirgsjäger 1939-1945: Die große Bildchronik
by Motorbuch Verlag

For the largest selection of fine reference books on this and related subjects, please visit our website - **www.schifferbooks.com** - or call for a free catalog.

We are interested in hearing from authors with book ideas on related topics.

Published by Schiffer Publishing Ltd.
4880 Lower Valley Road
Atglen, PA 19310
Phone: (610) 593-1777
FAX: (610) 593-2002
E-mail: info@schifferbooks.com.
Visit our web site at: www.schifferbooks.com
Please write for a free catalog.
This book may be purchased from the publisher.
Please include $3.95 postage.
Try your bookstore first.

In Europe, Schiffer books are distributed by:
Bushwood Books
6 Marksbury Avenue
Kew Gardens
Surrey TW9 4JF
England
Phone: 44 (0) 20 8392-8585
FAX: 44 (0) 20 8392-9876
E-mail: info@bushwoodbooks.co.uk.
Free postage in the UK. Europe: air mail at cost.
Try your bookstore first.

Contents

Introduction

Under the emblem of the edelweiss, the German mountain troops fought on all of the Second World War's many fronts—in the tundra of Lapland, in the hills and valleys of the Balkans, on Crete, in the Caucasus Mountains, at Monte Cassino and ultimately in Upper Italy and in the Western Alps, at the Semmering, and in Bavaria and Tyrol. Mountain troops even formed part of Rommel's *Afrikakorps*. By 1945 the army had formed a total of 11 mountain divisions, plus independent battalions and other units. Today the accomplishments of the "Men of the Edelweiss" are held in high regard by historians and military experts, and armed services and specialist units worldwide take their alpine and combat capabilities as an example. In mountain fighting bad weather and the difficult conditions often caused more casualties than the enemy.

The first comprehensive photo chronicle of the German mountain troops, this book uses impressive photographs and brief but insightful text to give the reader an inside look at the world of these elite troops, who were often committed where the situation was most critical. The book does not glorify war; instead, its purpose is to objectively depict where and how the German and Austrian mountain troops fought in the years 1939 to 1945.

I wish to express my thanks and appreciation to those who helped bring this book to fruition. I especially wish to thank my publisher, Dr. Patricia Scholten-Pietsch, for including the work in her company's program, my proofreader Martin Benz for editing the manuscript and the capable employees of Motorbuch Verlag and Frau Silvia Lechner for producing the computer layout.

Roland Kaltenegger
Kufstein, Tyrol, spring 2002

The Mountain Troops of the *Wehrmacht*

Following defeat in the First World War, the armies of the German kingdoms and principalities were disbanded.* Among them was the Royal Bavarian Army, and the German Alpine Corps was directly affected. It had fought extremely well in every theater, however, and the Army Command was determined it should again have mountain troops, despite the restrictions imposed by the Treaty of Versailles.

During the *Reichswehr* period, the lessons learned in the Great War and the spirit and traditions of the first German mountain corps were kept alive by the *III. (Gebirgs-Jäger) Bataillon* of *Infanterie-Regiment 19*, based in Kempten. For about a decade and a half this single battalion, together with the *II. (Gebirgs-Artillerie) Abteilung* based in Landsberg, a unit of the Munich-based *Artillerie-Regiment 7*, formed the *Reichswehr*'s entire mountain corps. The elite of mountain artillery, mountain climbing, and skiing were concentrated in these units.

Soon, however, storm clouds again appeared on the horizon. In response to the reintroduction of mandatory service in France, on 16 March 1935 Germany passed the "Law for the Building Up of the Armed Services." Compulsory military service was reintroduced, and the restrictions on armaments imposed by the Treaty of Versailles were declared invalid. A law governing military service was passed on 21 May 1935, and on 24 August a two-year period of military service was introduced. The *Reichsheer der Reichswehr* (National Army of the National Armed Services) was to be expanded to a total of 36 divisions organized in 12 army corps. The name *Reichswehr* was replaced by *Wehrmacht*.

The Austrian question resulted in political tension between National-Socialist Germany and Fascist Italy, and there were consequences for the mountain corps. In June 1935 a complete mountain brigade was formed from the few mountain units of the 100,000-man army that bore the stamp of its former commander Seeckt. The brigade included newly-formed units and elements of the Bavarian State Police with mountain experience. It was commanded by *Oberst* Ludwig Kübler, one of the founders of the German mountain troops.

The brigade headquarters was located in the old Bavarian war ministry in Munich, which also housed representatives of the corps headquarters of the *VII. Armeekorps*. Most of the mountain brigade was quartered in modern new barracks in the magnificent Alpine country of Bavaria and the Allgäu Region. In the spring of 1938 the mountain brigade was expanded to become the *1. Gebirgs-Division*.

Following the *Anschluss*, the incorporation of Austria into the German Reich, existing headquarters and units were used to form the *2. Gebirgs-Division* in Innsbruck and the *3. Gebirgs-Division* in Graz. German troops were added to both divisions, which were attached to the newly-established *XVIII. Gebirgs-Armeekorps* in Salzburg, rather than the *VII. Armeekorps* in Munich. Within the mountain troops and in German propaganda the mountain army corps was immediately dubbed the "Alpine Corps." The mountain troops were garrisoned in the beautiful towns of Kempten, Sonthofen, and Füssen in the Allgäu Region, and picturesque Murnau, Oberammergau, Garmisch-Partenkirchen, Mittenwalde, Lenggries, Brannenburg am Inn, Laufen an der Salzach, Bad Reichenhall, and Berchtesgaden in Upper Bavaria. To them were now added beautifully situated garrisons in *Ostmark* (Austria), in the regions of Vorarlberg, Tyrol, Salzburg, Carinthia, and Styria.

The outbreak of war in 1939 hindered the planned reorganization of the German mountain troops and had other serious effects. Mountain and winter combat training by the newly-formed units was seriously curtailed as a result of mobilization and the fighting in Poland. There was also a shortage of reserves. Worse

---

*There was no Imperial Army, just an Imperial Navy. Nevertheless, the armies were under a unified supreme command.

still, the bulk of the large mountain formations created during the Second World War were based on a cadre of personnel drawn from the original three divisions. Their replacement training units were drawn in, and the third mountain infantry regiment, so vital in combat, was eliminated. This meant that the mountain divisions had just two core units, unlike the panzer divisions, which had three. In spite of this, during the course of the Second World War, not only did the responsible generals establish and commit additional potent mountain units, they created the largest mountain corps in history, one whose striking power was unequalled.

At the end of the six-year civil war the armed services of Greater Germany had at their disposal the *Gebirgs-Armee-Oberkommando 20* (mountain army high command), the *XV., XVIII., XIX., XXI., XXII., XXXVI., XXXXIX.,* and *LI. Gebirgs-Armeekorps* (mountain army corps), the *1.* to *10.* and *188. Gebirgs-Division* (mountain divisions), and other mountain units. Among these were *Gebirgs-Jäger-Regiment 756* (mountain infantry regiment), the *2. Gebirgs-Jäger-Kompanie/Sonderverband 288* (mountain infantry company/special unit), *Heeres Gebirgs-Jäger-Bataillone 201* and *202* (army mountain infantry battalions), *Gebirgs-Beobachtungs-Abteilung 38* (mountain observation battalion), *Gebirgs-Beobachtungs-Batterien 23* and *73* (mountain observation batteries), *Gebirgs-Korps-Nachrichten-Abteilung 449* (mountain corps signals battalion), *Heeres-Gebirgs-Pionier-Bataillone 74, 85* and *818* (army mountain pioneer battalions), *Gebirgs-Nachschub-Kolonnen-Abteilungen 99* and *100* (mountain supply column battalions), *Gebirgs-Träger-Bataillone 54, 55, 56, 57, 67, 68* and *94,* (mountain carrier battalions), *Kriegsgefangenen-Gebirgs-Träger-Bataillon 54* (POW mountain carrier battalion), *(Gebirgs)-Radfahr-Bataillon 402* (mountain bicycle battalion), *Polizei-Gebirgs-Jäger-Regiment 18* (police mountain infantry regiment), *Gebirgs-Jäger Regiment Admoni, Heeres-Gebirgs-Jäger-Bataillon Allgäu, Jäger-Division Alpen, Sonderverband "Bergmann," Gebirgs-Jäger-Brigade 139 "Generaloberst Dietl"* (mountain infantry brigade), *Bataillon "Heine"* (reserve mountain infantry battalion), *Gebirgs-Jäger-Regiment Meeralpen, Gebirgs-Jäger-Division Steiermark, Gebirgs-Jäger-Regiment Treeck,* the *turkestanischen Gebirgs-Träger-Bataillone 1000* and *1001,* the *Hochgebirgs-Jäger-Bataillone 1, 2, 3* and *4* (high-mountain infantry battalions), and the *Skijäger-Regimenter* (ski infantry regiments), which were ultimately combined in the *1. Skijäger-Division.*

In Scandinavia, the Balkans and, at the end of the war, on the Upper Rhine and Semmering, the army's mountain troops were ably supported by two command agencies and six mountain divisions of the *Waffen-SS.* They were: *Generalkommando V. SS-Gebirgs-Korps* (corps headquarters) and Headquarters, *IX. Waffen-Gebirgs-Korps,* plus the *6. SS-Gebirgs-Division "Nord,"* the *7. SS-Freiwilligen-Gebirgs-Division "Prinz Eugen"* (mountain volunteer division), the *13. Waffen-Gebirgs-Division "Handschar" (kroatische Nr. 1),* the *21. Waffen-Gebirgs-Division der SS "Skanderberg" (albanische Nr. 1),* the *23. Waffen-Gebirgs-Division der SS "Kama" (kroatische Nr. 2),* and the *24 Waffen-Gebirgs-Division der SS "Karstjäger".* Although the mountain infantry of the *Waffen-SS* are not the actual subject of our documentation, we will encounter elite troops wearing the Edelweiss and the Death's Head in many theaters. There is good reason for this, for the mountain units of the *Wehrmacht* and the *Waffen-SS* were frequently interlinked. Mountain units of the *Waffen-SS* were attached to mountain units of the army and vice versa, and at times this interlinking was such that the two literally merged into a single corps. This unique relationship resulted in a special sense of trust between the mountain troops of the *Wehrmacht* and the *Waffen-SS,* which was characterized by mutual respect and recognition, and has lasted until the present day. It is not without good reason, for example, that the mountain troops of the *9. Gebirgs-Division,* a mixed *Wehrmacht* and *Waffen-SS* unit, and the veterans association of the *6. SS-Gebirgs-Division "Nord"* were welcomed into the circle of comrades of the former mountain troops in the 1950s and remain members to the present day.

The Mountain Divisions

The *1. GEBIRGS-DIVISION* was the founding division of the German mountain troops. Its bases stretched from the Allgäu Region across the Werdenfelser Land and the Chiemgau to the Berchtesgaden Land. It was formed under the well-known *General* Ludwig Kübler, and its longtime commander was *General* Hubert Lanz. He was followed by *Generale* Walter Stettner Ritter
von Grabenhofen, Josef Kübler, and August Wittmann. Galician Lvov and the French Oise-Aisne Canal, Yugoslavia, and the Ukraine, the breaching of the Stalin Line, the battle of encirclement at Uman and Podvysokoye, the capture of the Donets Region, the battles at Kharkov and Barvenkovo, the Caucasus and Kuban, the Balkans and the Ionian islands of Corfu and Cefalonia, Belgrade, and Lake Balaton—all are markers on the division's fateful path to the "Alpine Redoubt."

The *2. GEBIRGS-DIVISION* was the major mountain formation from the Tyrol-Vorarlberg District. It maintained a grand old Austrian tradition, recalling the excellent imperial light infantry and riflemen. Its ranks nevertheless included many Reich Germans. Its first commander was the Austrian *General* Valentin Feurstein. He was followed by *Generale* Ernst Schlemmer, Georg
Ritter von Hengl, Hans Degen, and Willibald Utz. The division took part in the fighting in Poland and Norway, "Operation Buffalo" in relief of the troops at Narvik, the four-year struggle in the tundra and on the Polar Sea near Murmansk, the defensive fighting in Lapland, the retreat to Norway as part of "Operation Northern Light," and the final battles in the south of the Reich and on the northern flank of the "Alpine Redoubt."

The *3. GEBIRGS-DIVISION* was the major mountain formation from Styria and Carinthia, bolstered by men from Bavaria. Its best-known commander was *General* Eduard Dietl. He was followed by *Generale* Julius Ringel, Hans Kreysing, Egbert Picker, August Wittmann, and Paul Klatt. From southern Poland, the division's path took it by
way of the Westwall (Siegfried Line) to the far north of Norway where, during the grueling struggle for Narvik, it caused the world to hold its breath. It subsequently participated in the fighting on the Liza, at Velikiye Luki, Millerovo, and Melitopol. From Nikopol it took part in the bitter retreat through the Ukraine, across the Dniepr, Ingulets, Bug and Dnestr Rivers, across the Carpathians, and through Hungary to Olmütz.

The *4. GEBIRGS-DIVISION* combined men from Wurttemberg, Baden, Bavaria, Austria, and South Tyrol. It was founded in 1940 under the Austrian *General* Eglseer, who later died in a plane crash in Styria, together with the legendary *General* Dietl. He was followed as commander by *Generale* Hermann Kress, Julius Braun, and Friedrich
Breith. After the campaign in the Balkans, the "Gentian Division" fought exclusively on the Eastern Front, from the first day of the Russian campaign to the last. The high points of its battle calendar were Lvov (Lemberg) and the Stalin Line, Vinnitsa and Uman, the Donets Region and the Mius River, the mountains and forests of the Caucasus, Novorossisk and Myshako Mountain, the Kuban bridgehead and the Crimean Peninsula, the Nogay Steppe and Kherson, the Carpathians and the High Tatra, plus Ungvar and Olmütz. It traveled no less than 10 800 kilometers and left behind an equal number of dead.

The *5. GEBIRGS-DIVISION* consisted of men from Upper and Lower Bavaria, men from the Bavarian forests, and Ostmark (Austria). Its founder and longtime commander was the Austrian *General* Julius Ringel. He was followed by *Generale* Max Schrank and Hans Steets. Among the battles fought by the "Chamois Division" were the Metaxas Line in Greece and the
Mediterranean island of Crete, at Lake Ladoga and the Volkhov River in Russia. The division late fought at Monte Cassino and Rimini in Italy, and in the western Alps on Mont Blanc and St. Bernhard. Its battle cry was "Hurrah the Chamois!"

The *6. GEBIRGS-DIVISION* combined men from Austria and South Tyrol with Sudeten and Reich Germans. It was hurriedly established in 1940 by Ferdinand Schörner, who later went into history as Hitler's "Last-Minute Field Marshal." Schörner's iron will left an indelible mark on the division throughout its existence. Subsequent commanders

were *Generale* Christian Philipp and Max-Josef Pemsel. The "Sixth" fought in the Vosges during the French campaign, then at the Metaxas Line, Mount Olympus and Thermopylae in Greece. Elements of the division also took part in the invasion of Crete. It later fought on the Polar Sea near Murmansk before it was forced to retreat to Norway with the remaining German forces in the north. Its motto "The Arctic is Nothing!" was originated by Schörner in 1941-42, when the division successfully fought far superior enemy forces to a standstill in the frozen tundra.

The *7. GEBIRGS-DIVISION* had its origins in the *99. leichte Infanterie-Division*, which in 1941 fought its way across the Dniepr to the Ukrainian capital of Kiev. During the winter of 1941-42 the Bavarian-Frankish division was transferred to the Grafenwöhr troop training grounds, where it was brought up to strength through the addition of Austrian units and reorganized as  a mountain division. At the beginning of 1942 elements of the division fought in front of Leningrad at Lake Ilmen and Lake Ladoga, while others were deployed near Uchta in Karelia. Then, in the summer of 1942, all units of the division were brought together on the Finnish front at Kiestinki. After Finland's ceasefire in the autumn of 1944, the "Climbing Boot Division" retreated through Rovaniemi to Norway as part of "Operation Birch." The division was commanded by *General* Kurt von der Chevallerie, the veteran Austrian artillery officer, *General* Robert Martinek, and the German *General* August Krakau.

The *8. GEBIRGS-DIVISION* was originally established as the *157. Reserve-Division* in *Wehrkreis VII* (Munich). It was later renamed the *157. Division*, and finally the *8. Gebirgs-Division*. The division was commanded by *Generale* Karl Pflaum and Diplom-Ingenieur Paul Schricker. From 1942-1944 the 157. Reserve-*Division* was used as an occupation unit in the Grenoble  area. As the *8. Gebirgs-Division* it subsequently fought in the French western Alps on Mont Blanc, on Petit St. Bernhard and on Mont Cenis, guarding the Alpine passes. The division also fought in the Appennines at Monte Sole, Monte Rumici, and Monte Adone against an enemy five times its strength. It later saw action south of Bologna, on Lake Garda and in the Etsch Valley in the "Alpine Foothills" and "Alpine Redoubt" areas of operation.

The *9. GEBIRGS-DIVISION* was created in the final weeks of the war, first as "Battle Group Semmering," also known as "Battle Group Raithel." The unit's personnel were a mixture of *Wehrmacht* and *Waffen-SS* training units and air force and navy personnel. Under *Oberst* Heribert Raithel, this thrown-together unit defended large sectors of the incomplete "Alpine Redoubt" against the onslaught of the Red Army.

The 10. *GEBIRGS-DIVISION* was formed in Lapland in March-April 1944 as "Division Group Kräutler," from the reinforced *Gebirgs-Jäger-Regiment 139*, *General* Dietl's legendary "Narvik Regiment," and other units with mountain experience. The Austrian *General* Mathias Kräutler was its founder and commander. He led his troops among the lakes and marshes of the primeval  Karelian forest. As part of "Operation Birch" the division took the second line of retreat from central Finland through the covering position at Rovaniemi to Norway.

The *188. GEBIRGS-DIVISION* was originally *Division Nr. 188*, which for a long time served as the replacement training division of Headquarters, *XVIII. Gebirgs-Armeekorps* in Salzburg. In 1944, as the *188. Reserve-Gebirgs-Division*, it was deployed as an occupation unit in northern Italy and in the "Adriatic Coast" operations zone, defending the coast from Isonzo  through Trieste to Fiume on Istria. The division engaged in heavy fighting with Italian, but especially Yugoslavian, partisan units. Even on the evening before the surrender it was given an offensive assignment against Allied forces far superior in numbers. The division was commanded by *Generale* Ernst Schlemmer and Hans von Hößlin.

Division emblems of the Mountain
units of the *Waffen*-SS:

6. SS-Gebirgs-Division "Nord"

*7. SS-Freiwilligen-Gebirgs-Division
"Prinz Eugen"*

*13. Waffen-Gebirgs-Division der SS
"Handschar"*

*21. Waffen-Gebirgs-Division der SS
"Skanderberg"*

*24. Waffen-Gebirgs-Division der SS
"Karstjäger"*

*Right: Swearing-in of recruits in
Garmisch-Partenkirchen during the
winter months. The assembled officers, non-commissioned officers, and
enlisted men wear the winter coat with
belt and steel helmet. Looming in the
background are the Wetterstein
Mountains with the Zugspitze massif.*

*The Waffen-SS also formed five mountain divisions dur-
ing the war, two of which were made up largely of foreign
volunteers. Above the emblems of the 6. SS-Gebirgs-Division "Nord," the 7. SS-Freiwilligen-Gebirgs-Division
"Prinz Eugen" (mainly ethnic Germans from Transylvania
and the Banat), the 13. Waffen-Gebirgs-Division der SS
"Handschar" (mainly Croatian and Bosnian volunteers),
the 21. Waffen-Gebirgs-Division der SS "Skanderberg"
(Albanian volunteers, division named after the Albanian
national hero), and the 24. Waffen-Gebirgs-Division der
SS "Karstjäger."*

Swearing-in of mountain troops in Garmisch-Partenkirchen: "I swear to God this sacred oath, that as a brave soldier I […] will be ready at any time to risk my life for this oath."

14

Above: A battalion of mountain infantry assembled on a **Heldengedenktag** *(equivalent of Memorial Day) in March. Below: Guests and spectators follow the swearing-in ceremony. In the background are the Wetterstein Mountains with the Zugspitze massif, the Waxensteinen, and the Alpspitze (from right to left).*

General *Ludwig Kübler, founder of the German mountain corps.*

A "robust mountain infantryman" making music.

17

The Mountain Corps' Peacetime Bases

Entrance to the barracks complex in Garmisch-Partenkirchen.

Barracks complex in Mittenwald.

The Carpathian Barracks in Sonthofen, with view of the Allgäu Alps.

Above: The mountain infantry barracks near Berchtesgaden. Below: The barracks complex in Bad Reichenhall.

Mountain cabins of the founding division of the German Mountain Corps.

The Schwarzenkopf Cabin (1336 m) above Lake Spitzing, in the Bavarian Alps.

The Ehrwalder Alm (1575 m) in Tyrol.

The Wimbachgrieß Cabin in the Berchtesgaden Alps, with members of Gebirgs-Jäger-Regiments 100 *during winter battle training in January 1936.*

Mountain infantry climbing with ski poles. The branches would be used to build positions.

Gebirgsjäger *during a high mountain exercise in their element—mountains of rock and ice.*

Above: Mountain infantry on the western peak of the Karwendel.

Left: Practicing roping down of wounded or injured soldiers using the Dülfer Seat. Note the tapered mountain pants with ankle wrap putties, which were known as "Ankle Sharpening Strips," and the characteristic boots worn by the mountain troops.

Below: Mountain infantry and artillery enter neighboring Tyrol during the incorporation of Austria into the German Reich in spring 1938.

Mounted flag party from a mountain infantry battalion with its banner during the peaceful entry into Austria.

In the gaily-decorated Tyrolean fortress city of Kufstein after the Anschluss: a mountain infantry officer takes the marchpast of his unit.

Kufstein: a mountain infantry company marches out on a formal occasion.

General *Eduard Dietl during an inspection of troops in the Franz-Josef Barracks in Graz.*

After the bloodless Anschluss the **Wehrmacht***'s mountain troops also began using Austrian high mountain training areas—here the Wattener Lizum.*

Mountain soldiers raised the Reich war flag on the 3797-meter-high Grossglockner, the highest peak in the Greater German Reich. In the background the snow-covered Hohen Tauern.

Mountain training in the Alpine lake valleys.

Soldiers receive climbing instruction in the field. Note the tapered mountain pants worn by the soldier on the left, and the breeches and climbing boots worn by **General Rudolf Konrad** *on the right.*

Above: Little snow for ski training in the Alps near Kitzbühl. In the background the Wilde Kaiser.

Right: A ski platoon during a winter exercise in the Karwendel Mountains. The soldiers are wearing snow smocks, used only by mountain troops in peacetime.

Below: Ski training in the snow-covered Alps. Some of the instructors are wearing snow camouflage suits.

This photograph shows an NCO with the high-mountain clothing and equipment typically used by the mountain troops. He wears the windbreaker introduced in 1938, made of impregnated woven cloth. The windbreaker was reversible, with white and gray sides; here the white side is out. This Gebirgsjäger is also wearing a white cotton liner over the typical mountain cap, together with tinted snow goggles. Mounted on his Type 31 rucksack for high mountain troops are a climbing rope, an ice axe, and snowshoes; resting on the man's right shoulder are his skis. Slung round his neck is a Maschinenpistole 40 submachine-gun and a pair of 6 x 30 binoculars.

Equipment, Weapons, & Tools
An Overview

Almost every branch of the army was represented in the mountain troops. A mountain division could thus carry out the same missions as infantry or light infantry divisions. The mountain corps encompassed the three main branches of the army: mountain infantry, mountain artillery, and mountain pioneers. There were others as well: signals units, anti-tank units, reconnaissance units, and supply. The mountain soldiers of these branches obviously had to be up to the greater physical demands of mountain service and be familiar with the unique conditions in the mountains, but they also needed to be better equipped to be able to fulfill their often difficult combat assignments.

The *Wehrmacht*'s mountain troops wore the uniform of the German Army. It consisted of a gray tunic or similarly-colored blouse with field gray trousers. The collar patches, piping, braid, cuff patches, etc worn by the mountain infantry were in the service color light green. Those of the mountain artillery were bright red, and the mountain pioneers black, while the signals troops wore lemon yellow collar and cuff patches. The mountain troops also had certain attributes that distinguished them from the other services. One was the mountain cap with the metal edelweiss emblem on the left side; the standard army garrison cap introduced in 1943 was patterned after this cap. Another was the uniform worn by the mountain troops, which made it possible for breeches to be worn with heavy woolen socks and climbing boots, ski pants with ski boots, or trousers with putties and climbing boots. Other specialized clothing worn by mountain troops included windbreakers and camouflage clothing, such as snow smocks, snow suits, and snow camouflage overalls, snow and camouflage masks, as well as climbing shoes, whose soles were fitted with hobnails. A reversible anorak with wind pants proved very effective. No less effective was the *Wehrmacht* climbing boot. Personal equipment included breeches, woolen sweaters, and various items to guard against heat, weather, sun, and rain.[1]

31

Nevertheless, the mountain equipment was, to use a word coined by *Generaloberst* Eduard Dietl, "journeyman-like." In general it was designed to suit the function, the service, the mission, and the time of year. It therefore differed from summer to winter, but differences in flat and mountainous terrain were less significant. In addition to the characteristic rucksack, the mountain soldier's equipment also included special clothing for winter and summer.

In addition to the army's specialist badges and special duty badges, for soldiers who carried out a special function or had taken special training—for example, fire fighter, technical sergeant, horseshoeing instructor, and many more—there were three army qualification badges in the mountain corps. They included the Edelweiss Badge for mountain guides and, with restrictions, the Ski Infantry Badge. The authorized strength of a mountain division was:

Approximately 14,000 men and 5,000 to 6,000 animals, of which about 1,500 were horses, 4,300 pack animals, and 550 mountain horses, which were used mainly as pack animals. 1,400 vehicles (including automobiles and motorcycles), plus 660 horse-drawn vehicles. Weapons: 13,000 rifles, 2,200 pistols, 500 machine-guns, 416 light machine-guns, 66 light mortars, 75 anti-tank rifles, 80 heavy machine-guns, 44 medium mortars, 16 light infantry guns, 4 heavy infantry guns, 39 anti-tank guns, 12 light anti-aircraft guns, 24 light mountain guns, 12 light field or mountain howitzers, and 12 heavy howitzers.

In general, the *Gebirgsjäger*'s mountain equipment was adapted to suit his current functions, operational role, and time of year. Logically, it differed from summer to winter, though in flat terrain it was not so different than in the high mountains.

Camouflage smocks and snowsuits made the troops difficult for the enemy to see in snow-covered mountains or ice-covered regions. Snow goggles protected the eyes and were needed to prevent snow blindness. The compass was a basic item of equipment for any independent unit operating in the mountains, and binoculars for every unit leader. The mountain rucksack and mountain boots were, of course, basic items of equipment for every mountain soldier.

It was particularly important that the troops be provided with sufficient numbers of cooking pots, water containers, pack saddles, and back frames. Units produced their own pack saddles, saddle blankets, halters, pack baskets, and similar items in their own small workshops. Such activities were no proper replacement for organized, standard equipment, however.

Introduced in 1935, the *Karabiner 98k*, lighter and shorter than the *Gewehr 98* used in the First World War, performed magnificently as the standard weapon of the mountain troops in the Second World War. As the war went on, the mountain troops were issued various captured weapons and self-loaders, but none was able to completely replace the K 98k repeater.

The G-43 self-loader and the *Sturmgewehr 44* assault rifle were issued to the troops in significant numbers. The latter inspired German and Soviet designs in the postwar period.

Beginning in the autumn of 1940, many of the mountain units were issued the Gew 33/40 mountain carbine, a Czech-built weapon. The carbine's barrel was considerably shorter than that of the K 98k (49 cm vs 60 cm); consequently, recoil and muzzle flash were much stronger.

Rifles with telescopic sights were of particular importance to the mountain troops. They were issued various sniper versions of the K 98k, as well as other weapons, the Gewehr 33/40 with ZF 41 sight being the most important.

The mountain troops produced a number of outstanding snipers. Typical of these was Matthias Hetzenauer from Tyrol. He served on the Eastern Front from 1943 until the end of the war, and with 345 confirmed kills he was the most successful sniper of the Second World War.[2]

The l.MG 34 light machine-gun was used with success in the high mountains, as was the more robust MG 42. Even in the difficult conditions of the Polar Sea these weapons seldom jammed. The MG 34 could be used as a heavy machine-gun by placing it on a fixed mount. This improved accuracy and—thanks to the mount's angle of traverse—field of fire, making it more useful against shifting targets at longer ranges.

For close-range fighting the mountain troops used the P 08 and P 38 army pistols and the MP 38 and 40 submachine-guns, the latter being a mass-produced version of the former. Mountain troops fighting in Lapland and the Eastern Front made extensive use of the Russian PPsH 41 machine pistol, with its characteristic drum magazine holding 71 rounds of 7.62-mm ammunition.

Other close-range infantry weapons were the Type 24, 39, and 42 stick grenades, and the Type 39 eggshape hand grenade. For combating armored vehicles the mountain troops used the *Wehrmacht*'s standard anti-tank weapons: the 3-kg hollow charge; Type 35, 42, and 43 anti-tank mines; and, of course, various versions of the *Panzerfaust* and the *Panzerschreck*, the latter an 88-mm anti-tank rocket launcher.

For transport in marshy or mountainous regions, or areas where roads were few, the 20-mm *Flak 38* could be broken down into eight components that could be carried by pack animals. They were used with success against enemy aircraft, including in the high passes of the Caucasus and the Western Alps. The 20-mm *Gebirgsflak 38* was designed to be dropped by parachute and was intended for use by parachute and mountain troops. It was issued to the mountain troops in small numbers. The 50-mm *Granatwerfer 36* mortar weighed 14 kg and was easily transported, however, its range and the effectiveness of its projectiles proved inadequate. The 80-mm *Granatwerfer 34* (combat weight: 62 kg with steel barrel, 57 kg with light metal barrel) was better suited to the requirements of the mountain troops. The short-barreled *Granatwerfer 42* ("Stump Mortar," combat weight 26.5 kg) did not live up to expectations, however, its 81-mm mortar shells proving ineffective in snow-covered terrain and on glaciers. As a result, the 120-mm *Granatwerfer 42*, based on Russian designs, was introduced in 1943. Also used in large numbers was the 120-mm *Granatwerfer 378(r)*, a Russian weapon captured in large numbers. Previously classed as a heavy mortar, the 80-mm weapon was redesignated as a medium mortar.

German anti-tank guns were found to be ineffective at the start of the Russian campaign. Using standard ammunition, the 37-mm Pak 35/36 posed no threat to the Soviet medium and heavy tanks. Guns and crews were often overrun. The situation did not improve until the introduction of the *Stielgranate 41*

with hollow-charge head for the 37-mm anti-tank gun, the 50-mm Pak 38 anti-tank gun, and later the effective 75-mm Pak 40.

Used by heavy companies and platoons, the Type 18 light (mountain) infantry gun proved especially effective for placing high-angle fire on targets behind cover, and because of its caliber (105-mm) it also had a great effect on morale. The units also received a wide variety of other mountain guns, from the 75-mm *Gebirgsgeschütz 36* to the 105-mm Type 322(f) light mountain howitzer. A description of all these weapons would exceed the scope of this work.[3]

Stocks of ammunition were of vital importance. The old saying went that the effectiveness in combat of a mortar, gun, or rifle was only as great as the amount of ammunition available. Special emphasis was therefore placed on allocating sufficient quantities of ammunition, for a few mountain mortars and guns with plenty of ammunition were far better than the reverse. Ammunition for mortars and guns was loaded onto trucks and then unloaded and transported as required.

Mountain units had to possess the optimum balance between combat power and mobility, for even the best-equipped unit is of little use if it cannot reach decisive sectors in time. Like the other arms, the mountain troops relied on a vast array of motor vehicles. The following are only examples:

The NSU Opel tracked motorcycle (*Kettenkrad*) with trailer could transport loads up to 700 kg. Average fuel consumption was 25 liters per 100 kilometers. The narrow track and excellent maneuverability made it possible for the vehicle to drive through dense undergrowth. Its climbing ability was less impressive, however. The VW *Kübelwagen*, like the 2-5-ton standard diesel, was a light, off-road vehicle. There was a variety of half-tracked vehicles in the 1.3- to 8-ton class applicable to the mountain troops. The Steyr A 1500 (Kfz 69) was used as a command vehicle. The three-ton Mercedes L 3000 and Opel Blitz were both medium trucks with off-road capability. There were two basic types of horse-drawn vehicle—four-wheel army field wagons and two-wheel carts—that could carry loads up to 350 kg and be pulled by a single horse. They proved particularly useful, especially with rubber tires.[4]

Skis proved indispensable as a means of transport in the snow-covered mountains, as well as in the Arctic and Russia during the winter. For crossing rocky areas or glaciers the troops required specialized alpine equipment, such as ropes, picks, climbing shoes, avalanche ropes, and snow tires. Four-pointed light crampons sufficed for normal movement on glaciers. Ten- or 12-pointed crampons were only required for particularly difficult ice conditions.

Notes:

[1] See *Die deutsche Wehrmacht, Uniformierung und Ausrüstung 1933-1945, Band 1: Das Heer*, written by Adolf Schlicht and John R. Angolia (Motorbuch Verlag, 4th Edition, Stuttgart 2000). A brilliant color depiction of several mountain troops with equipment is found in *Deutsche Uniformen 1939-1945* by Jean de Lagarde (Motorbuch Verlag, 2nd Edition, Stuttgart 1999).

[2] The story of German snipers is told in detail by Peter Senich in *Deutsche Scharfschützenwaffen 1939-1945* (Motorbuch Verlag, Stuttgart 1996).
Those with a special interest in the telescopic sights used with the 98k carbine can turn to *K 98k als Scharfschützenwaffe* (Motorbuch Verlag/Verlag Stocker-Schmid, Stuttgart/Dietikon-Zurich, 1998).

The *Enzyklopädie deutscher Waffen 1939-1945* by Terry Gander and Peter Chamberlain (Motorbuch Verlag 1999) is an outstanding survey of all German small arms, artillery and special weapons, including captured equipment, of the Second World War.

[3] The *Enzyklopädie deutscher Waffen 1939-1945* (see above) devotes an entire chapter to mountain guns.

[4] The various horse-drawn vehicles are described in *Die bespannten Truppen der Wehrmacht* by Klaus Christian Richter (Motorbuch Verlag, Stuttgart 1997).
A further description of these vehicles was written by Wolfgang Fleischer and appeared in Waffen-Arsenal Vol. 153: *Deutsche Infanteriekarren, Heeresfeldwagen und Heeresschlitten 1900-1945* (Podzun-Pallas Verlag, Wölfersheim 1995).

The senior NCO of a mountain infantry company collects from his men for the **Winterhilfswerk** *(winter relief fund). He is wearing the mountain cap, which has a smaller peak than the standard garrison cap introduced in 1943. On the left side is the stamped Edelweis emblem of the mountain troops made of oxidized silver. The "Jäger" proudly wear the sleeve badge of the mountain troops on the upper right sleeve of their tunics. It and the metal cap badge were introduced in May 1939. The emblems had their origins in the German Alpine Corps of the First World War.*

34

Oberjäger of the Gebirgs-Pionier-Bataillon 54 of the
1. Gebirgs-Division *wearing tunic, mountain cap, and the Marksmanship Fourragère, 2nd to 4th Class.*

Classic photograph of a mountain infantryman. It appeared as a color postcard shortly before the outbreak of war.

Gliederung eines Geb.Jg.Rgt. · Seine Stärke u. Bewaffnung

Einheit	Nummerierung	Takt.Zeich.	Offz. u.o.m.	Tragt.	Fahrz.	LKW/PKW	Kräd.	J.G.	GrW s	GrW l	MG s	MG l	Pak
Rgt.-Stab	98		50	3 (7)		7 (1)	8						
Rgt.-N.3.			81	21 (1)			1						
(Pak)-Kp.	16		170			5 (36)	31					4	12
l.Inf.Kol.(mot.)			47			16 (2)	3						
Btl.-Stab	III II I		40	5 (11)		2 (1)	5						
Geb.Jäger Kp.	11. 6. 1.		229	40 (10)	4	4	2			3	2	9	
"	12. 7. 2.		229	40 (10)	4	4	2			3	2	9	
"	13. 8. 3.		229	40 (10)	4	4	2			3	2	9	
(Schwere)G.Jäg.Kp.	14. 9. 4.		272	96 (23)	4	4	4	2	6				
(Stabs)-Kp.	15. 10. 5.		244	53 (16)	5	7	7				4		
Jetzige Gesamtstärken des Btl.:			1243	354	21	25 (1)	22	2	6	9	10	27	
Frühere Gesamtstärke (zum Vergleich):			1090	249	34	13	7	—	—	—	12	27	
Jetzige Gesamtstärke des Rgt:			4077	1094	63	103 (42)	109	6	18	27	30	85	12
Frühere Gesamtstärke (zum Vergleich):			3729	803	112	46 (45)	58	6	—	—	36	85	12

Table depicting the organization, strength, and armament of a mountain infantry regiment.

36

The submachine-gun and binoculars formed part of the equipment of patrol, squad, and platoon leaders. Note the bag worn around the neck for carriage of stick-type hand grenades.

Gliederung einer Geb. Jäger Kompanie

Komp. Trupp
15 KÖPFE 2 REITPFERDE 4 TRAGTIERE

3 Züge zu je:

1 Zugtr. 1 l.Gr.W.Tr. und
7 KÖPFE   5 KÖPFE 2 TRAGTIERE

3 Gruppen zu je:
100, 4 MG-S.   6 SCH.,   2 TRAGTIERE

S.M.G.-Gr.
19 KÖPFE   6 TRAGTIERE

Gefechtstross:

a. Bergstaffel
6 TRAGTIERE VERPFL. WASSER FUTTER   2 FELDKÜCHEN

b. Talstaffel
15 KRAD 2 LKW

Verpflegungstross
2 VERPFL.-FAHRZEUGE

Gepäcktroß
1 mKRAD 2 LKW
GERÄT   GEPÄCK

Organization and strength of mountain infantry company.

Above: Equipment for use in the high mountains: Type 31 rucksack, steel helmet for protection against falling rock, rope, and ice axe.

Left: The snow smock allowed the Gebirgsjäger *to literally blend into a snow-covered mountain.*

Below: Two young mountain infantrymen wearing windbreakers. The man on the right is wearing the gray side out, the man on the right the white.

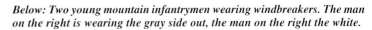

Twelve-point crampons for negotiating glaciers and icy paths.

During winter or in the high mountains, tents consisting of four Type 31 tent squares fastened together were used to provide some protection against the wind and cold.

40

Rocky nests high in the mountains were almost impossible for an opponent to storm. The carriage-mounted heavy machine-gun increased the defensive strength of these isolated positions considerably. This photograph was taken during an exercise in 1939, which is confirmed by the absence of the Edelweis emblem on the mountain caps.

Mountain infantry with a sMG 34 heavy machine-gun in a cotton field in Russia, 1941.

Carrying small arms and full ammunition boxes, mountain troops advance on the enemy. Third from the left is **General** *Lanz,* *commanding officer of the* **1. Gebirgs-Division.**

Gebirgsjäger with Gewehr 33/40 rifle on the Mius River front in 1942.

Mountain infantry firing the P 38 and P 08 pistols in Luttensee above the Mittenwald. Members of the Hitler Youth and Luftwaffe auxiliaries were also permitted to take part.

Two-wheel horse-drawn mountain cart (Heeresfahrzeug 4) in ankle-deep Russian mud.

Four-wheel small field wagon (Heeresfahrzeug 3) in the southern sector of the Eastern Front.

44

Above: Command vehicles used by the mountain troops ranged from the light Volkswagen car through the Steyr A 1500 to Opel and Mercedes trucks.

Right: A Magirus-Deutz heavy prime mover.

Below: This rare photograph depicts the "Erlkönig" (Erl-king), a light utility vehicle built specially for the mountain troops.

Firing practice with the 75-mm Gebirgskanone 15. This weapon entered service with the Italian forces in 1915, and after the First World War was used by the armies of Austria, Bulgaria, Romania, Czechoslovakia, Hungary, and Turkey. Captured examples were issued to the German mountain troops. Though it was to have been superseded by the Gebirgsgeschütz 36, it soldiered on until 1945. Despite its age, it was one of the best mountain guns of the Second World War. Combat weight approx. 620 kg, maximum firing range 8250 meters.

Developed by Rheinmetall, the 75-mm Gebirgsgeschütz 36 was used with success by the mountain troops and was built by Wolf in Magdeburg from 1938 to 1944. Capable of being broken down into eight components for transport, it weighed approx. 750 kg and had a maximum range of 9250 meters.

Loading a 75-mm Gebirgsgeschütz 36 on one of eight pack animals.

Left: Firing demonstration by the 105-mm Leichtgeschütz 40 (LG 40), a recoilless weapon introduced in late 1941. The tow hook on the muzzle was used to attach the weapon to a towing vehicle. Combat weight approx. 430 kg, maximum range 8000 meters.

47

Transporting a 105-mm leichte Feldhaubitze 16 on a horse-drawn sledge. This weapon consisted of a First World War field howitzer on the carriage of the 75-mm Type 16 field gun. This was the first field gun issued to the artillery regiments in 1935. After 1939 it was used mainly by reserve and mountain infantry units. Combat weight approx. 1525 kg, maximum range 9225 meters. Note the gun's white winter camouflage finish, the white clothing worn by the crew, and the white horse blankets.

Anti-tank gunners move a 37-mm Type 35/36 anti-tank gun into position.

Captured during the campaign in France, Renault UE ammunition carriers, like the one illustrated here, were used by mountain troops to tow anti-tank guns.

The mountain troops also used the BMW R 12 heavy motorcycle with sidecar. The vehicles seen here belong to the motorcycle battalion of the 6. Gebirgs-Division. Note the edelweiss emblem on the rear of the sidecar.

Member of a mountain signals company with his pack animal in enemy territory. The mule's load consists in part of several reels of field telephone cable.

The Campaign Against Poland 1939

The all too brief period of peace came to an abrupt end on 1 September 1939, when war broke out with Poland. Two days later, on 3 September, England and France declared war on Germany. Only 13 infantry divisions were left in the west, under the command of *Generaloberst* Wilhelm Ritter von Leeb, while the bulk of the German Army—38 divisions, including four motorized, five armored, and all three mountain—were committed in an operation against western Poland.

The three mountain divisions, the "First" under *General* Kübler, the "Second" under *General* Feuerstein, and the "Third" under *General* Dietl, were deployed on the army's extreme right flank in the area of the Hohen Tatra and the hill and forest country of southeast Poland. They were under the overall command of *General der Infanterie* Eugen Beyer's *XVIII. Gebirgs-Armeekorps*. This mountain army corps, to which two infantry, one motorized, and one panzer division were attached at various times, had been given the task of smashing the extreme southern wing of the Polish Army and preventing the enemy from fleeing through the Lvov area to Hungary.

To accomplish this major task, *General* Kübler formed two motorized pursuit groups, one in the north and the other in the south. On 8 September they were committed to gain a crossing over the San River. The next day the southern group ran into stubbornly-defended Polish positions near Rymanow, which were assaulted and overcome. By the evening of 9 September Sambor was in German hands. The motorized mountain units, with their mountain infantry, mountain artillery, mountain pioneers, and all the other mountain soldiers, performed extremely well in numerous engagements and forced marches of 50 or more kilometers. They advanced so rapidly that they outpaced the unit on their left, the *2. Gebirgs-Division*, by about 100 km. This resulted in a dangerous gap. Ignoring this threat, the motorized groups charged ahead, sparing neither men, equipment, nor the tireless pack animals, and seized the suburbs of Lvov. This

51

daring, indeed reckless, charge, closed the Grodek narrows to the retreating Polish forces. There was fierce fighting, especially by the troops under *Oberst* Schörner near Zboiska and those under *Oberst* Utz at the Grodek narrows.

The efforts of the *XVIII. Gebirgs-Armeekorps* command were hampered by the loss of the *3. Gebirgs-Division*, which so far had seen only minor action and was engaged in trying to catch up. At the height of the battle for Lvov the division was taken away from the corps and diverted west into the Pfalz Forest. Nevertheless, the Galician capital fell after a bitterly-fought battle of encirclement that lasted nine days. In addition to preventing the Polish armies from escaping to the south, the units of the mountain army corps took 64,000 Polish prisoners and captured 110 guns and much equipment.

When Soviet troops suddenly appeared east of the city, having entered Poland in mid-September as per the terms of the pact between Hitler and Stalin, Polish negotiators offered to surrender the city to the *1. Gebirgs-Division*. It was too late, however, for in accordance with a secret protocol contained in the non-aggression pact between Germany and the Soviet Union, the unsuspecting mountain troops were obliged to leave the long-suffering population to the Red Army and withdraw beyond the agreed-upon demarcation line.

For the commanding general of the *XVIII. Gebirgs-Armeekorps*, who knew the Polish battlefields from the First World War, the victory at the Grodek narrows was the high point of his military career. During the victo-rious advance in France, Eugen Beyer was struck down by disease and died.

In recognition of his accomplishments in peace-time in building up the German mountain troops, and his *1. Gebirgs-Division*'s military success in the so-called, later much glorified "Dash to Lvov," *Generalmajor* Ludwig Kübler was awarded the Knight's Cross of the Iron Cross.

Warsaw was encircled on 11 September 1939 and, after sustained bombing, was occupied on 27 September. The campaign against Poland was the first demonstration of "Blitzkrieg," an entirely new type of warfare. Supported by air power, concentrations of armored forces broke through the enemy front at selected points, then attacked the enemy from behind, resulting in his encirclement and destruction.

In the meantime, *Generalmajor* Kübler read out to his troops the last division order of the day issued during the fighting in Poland. In it he thanked his courageous troops and coined the expression that was soon to become a dictum: "The Edelweiss has become the terror of the enemy!" But at what a cost! The *1. Gebirgs-Division*'s casualties during the 18 days of fighting totaled 1,402 men, including 47 officers, 76 NCOs, and 353 enlisted men killed.

Regretfully, we must conclude that because of lack of combat experience, misplaced elitist ideas, and Kübler's impetuous, indeed reckless, offensive tactics, the "Dash to Lvov" became the "Langemarck" of the founding division of the German mountain troops.

After this bloodletting, the "First" was temporarily incapable of further operations and had to be transferred to rest quarters to regain its strength.

Dispatch rider from Gebirgs-Jäger-Regiment 100 and Slovakian soldiers on the Polish-Slovakian border, 7 September 1939. Slovakia also entered the war, as Poland had earlier annexed Slovakian territory.

Studying the map.

Officers meet to discuss the situation.

Advance into southern Poland. Horse-drawn mountain artillery passes a line of advancing infantry.

German troops advancing on Lvov. The Red Army also moved in from the east, however, the "Protecting Powers" did not declare war on that nation.

The advance proceeds irresistibly in the late summer heat. Mountain troops and infantry cross a river over a ford of wooden beams.

The wrecked bridge in Prymysl.

Mountain artillery with their faithful pack animal.

Light field wagons proved effective, even with improvised harness.

Horsemen of the 1. Gebirgs-Division's reconnaissance battalion water their horses.

After endless kilometers in the hot sun, their boots snow-white from sand and dust, exhausted mountain troops rest by the side of a road.

Wrecked buildings in a Polish village.

59

Chimneys silhouetted against the sky are all that remain of a factory.

A unit of Gebirgs-Artillerie-Regiment 79 with its pack animals moves past knocked-out Polish tanks.

Further evidence of fierce fighting: a shot-up Krupp L2 H 143 truck.

Knocked-out Polish light tank.

German field kitchens shared their food with Polish civilians, especially children.

Advancing mountain infantry pass a column of Polish refugees.

Mountain infantry lead a column of Polish POWs to a collection point in the rear.

63

Collection point for Polish prisoners of war.

Heading home by train.

Marching into garrison after the 18-day campaign—in this case an Austrian police unit.

The Campaign in Norway

While the fighting raged in Poland and throughout the winter of 1939-40, the armies of the western powers sat on the west bank of the Rhine and behind the Maginot Line, the French fortification system. In the years between the wars the line was believed to be invulnerable to attack. During the first winter of the war the *1.*, *2.*, and *3. Gebirgs-Division* were stationed in the Rhineland, the Eifel Region, and the Ahr Valley. There the regiments and battalions trained in the snow-covered mountains, having received replacements from the training units to make good their initial losses. Before long, however, the *2.* and *3. Gebirgs-Division* were ordered to make preparations for a deployment to Scandinavia, leaving their motorized elements behind.

What was at stake? The Norwegian port of Narvik, through which flowed the bulk of the iron ore mined in Kiruna and Gällivare in northern Sweden, was of vital importance to German industry. Due to its own lack of mineral resources, Germany was (and is) dependent on imports of ore. The western powers were well aware of this, and Great Britain in particular was eager to take advantage of the situation. The result was an unprecedented race between the military forces of the two sides. Germany found itself forced to occupy Norway in order to secure the ice-free port of Narvik and the vital flow of iron ore. Great Britain and France, however, wanted to stop the flow of vital ore from Sweden to Germany. An Allied expeditionary force set sail for Scandinavia on 8 April 1940, before the Germans. One day later, after the enemy ships were discovered on the high sea, the *Wehrmacht* marched into Denmark and Norway. While tiny Denmark surrendered after the initial skirmishes—losing 11 killed—in Norway there was heavy fighting.

Aided by foggy weather, German naval units reached Norwegian waters, despite the presence of the mighty Home Fleet. After a rough voyage aboard 10 destroyers under the command of *Kapitän zur See* and *Kommodore* Friedrich Bonte, on 9 April the reinforced

Gebirgs-Jäger-Regiment 139 under *Generalmajor* Eduard Dietl landed at Narvik. The regiment lacked supplies, heavy weapons, pack animals, and vehicles of every kind. As a result, on 11 April, two days after the mountain troops went ashore, the commander of the 2nd Battery of *Gebirgs-Artillerie-Regiment 112* was ordered to fly to Narvik with 60 mountain artillerymen and four 75-mm mountain guns, plus the required ammunition. On arrival the battery would unload immediately, and during the night of 13 April attach itself to the "Windisch Group."

British battleships and cruisers sank all the German destroyers off Narvik, and *Kommodore* Bonte was killed. The mountain troops and surviving sailors were cut off. For the next two months there was costly fighting between encircled Germans and the far-superior Allies. The unequal struggle was marked by supply difficulties and harsh terrain. In April the situation of the Narvik fighters, facing about 25,000 well-equipped French and British troops, became critical, and Dietl considered a retreat to Swedish territory. In view of the impending German offensive in Western Europe and the launching of "Operation Buffalo," he instead decided to "hold out as long as possible."

What was "Operation Buffalo"? While the men at Narvik grimly defended their positions, elements of the *2. Gebirgs-Division* under *General* Feuerstein began fighting their way north from Trondheim, in central Norway, to relieve Battle Group Dietl. This meant an advance of about 1000 kilometers through mountainous terrain against stubborn resistance from Norwegian, British, and French forces. During the course of "Buffalo," a group of experienced mountain troops under *Oberstleutnant* Georg Ritter von Heng covered 200 kilometers of mountainous terrain with no roads. This "Buffalo" route—the land route between Sörfold and Narvik—first passed by way of Kroken through the Gjer Valley to Livsejovrre, then through Grunvfjordboin and the Gicce-Kokka glacier to Fjelbu, and from their to the ore railway that led to Narvik.

There the exhausted men of the *2.* and *3. Gebirgs-Division* linked up, while the Allies hastily withdrew on 8 June 1940 after their bitter defeat in France. Dietl, the "Hero of Narvik," entered the northern port city unopposed. More than that: after two promotions in rapid succession to the rank of *Generalleutnant* and first *General der Gebirgstruppe*, he also became the first member of the *Wehrmacht* to receive the newly created Knight's Cross of the Iron Cross with Oak Leaves. No fewer than seven members of *Gebirgs-Jäger-Regiment 139* were awarded the coveted Knight's Cross. But that was not all. In recognition of their "ordinary victory," all of those who fought at Narvik were decorated with the "Narvik Shield"—in silver for the army and air force, and gold for the navy.

The German troops had won the race to Scandinavia. It was a strategic operation, under the direct control of the *Wehrmacht* High Command. The British and French forces were forced to leave Norway, while the Norwegian forces, which in some cases had fought with determination, laid down their weapons. It should be mentioned that British losses would have been much heavier had German submarines had more reliable torpedoes. Many certain kills were lost because their so-called "detonator pistols" failed to function. This "torpedo crisis" resulted in a thorough investigation by the *Kriegsmarine*, but that is another story.

Cooperation between the three elements of the armed services (army, navy, and air force) had been almost flawless. More than 2,000 seaman whose ships had been sunk joined the ranks of the mountain troops, providing invaluable assistance in combat and noncombat roles. The *2.* and *3. Gebirgs-Division*, which had been sent to the far north, remained on the coast of the Polar Sea and prepared for their first Arctic winter.

Mountain infantry on board a German destroyer bound for Norway and an uncertain mission.

On board a northbound transport ship.

In Norwegian waters.

The transports near their port of destination.

Even the German mountain troops, accustomed to Alpine scenery, were caught up in the spell of the breathtaking fiord landscape.

Aftermath of the initial skirmishes.

*Opposite: Mountain infantry go ashore at Narvik. A painting
by Herbert Agricola.*

Sinking ships on the morning of 9 April 1940.

The aftermath of heavy fighting in the port of Narvik.

Ships' graveyard: Narvik after the German landing.

Daily ritual for the German soldier: the "Spiess" (top sergeant) of a mountain infantry company during morning prayers.

Right: Mountain infantry with ski equipment in Norway.

Below: Mountain artillery firing position. The weapons are 75-mm Gebirgskanonen 15 mountain cannon.

Exhausted dispatch rider. Note the soldier's mountain carbine. It is a Gewehr 33/40, which was issued mainly to mountain troops.

75-mm Gebirgsgeschütz 36 mountain gun in a concealed position by the ore railway. General Dietl called the mountain guns "Alpine Revolvers."

Above: Interesting photograph of the 75-mm Gebirgsgeschütz 36. Note the multi-chamber muzzle brake and sighting mechanism.
Below: Paratroopers were dropped from Ju 52 transports near Narvik. Here they are seen assembling and preparing for action.

General Eduard Dietl, commander of the 3. Gebirgs-Division, and General Valentin Feuerstein, commander of the 2. Gebirgs-Division, during an operations conference in Norway.

General Dietl with his "Flower Devils" following the successful conclusion of "Operation Buffalo." A battle group of mountain infantry covered 600 km (in a straight line) through the difficult high mountain terrain of the Arctic Circle to establish land communication with the surrounded forces at Narvik.

General der Gebirgsjäger Eduard Dietl, the "Hero of Narvik."

For his stubborn defense and ultimate victory at Narvik, in 1940 Hitler awarded General Dietl the first Knight's Cross with Oak Leaves.

A Feldwebel of the mountain troops wearing the Narvik Shield on his upper left sleeve. Created on 19 April 1940, the shield was only awarded to those members of the army, air force, and navy who participated directly in the Battle of Narvik (9 April to 9 June 1940). The shield for members of the army and air force was silver in color, while the navy's was gold. First presentation of the shield was to General Dietl by Adolf Hitler, Supreme Commander of the Armed Services, on 21 March 1941.

Following the conclusion of the Scandinavian campaign the mountain units were transported to the Polar Sea coast.

Toward the North Cape.

POLARCIRKEL
1937
At the Arctic Circle.

Mountain infantry on Reichsstrasse 50 to Alta-Kirkenes.

Road sign on Reichsstrasse 50.

The fallen stayed behind—German military cemetery in Norway.

A mountain unit's column of pack animals on the advance in France.

The French Campaign 1940

On 10 May 1940, while fighting was still going on at Narvik, three German army groups launched an offensive in the west. The main thrust was made by Army Group Center (also Army Group A, von Rundstedt) through southern Belgium and Luxembourg toward Sedan. The Maginot Line, thought to be impenetrable, was quickly breached by German panzer units. Within this army group was the *1. Gebirgs-Division* under *General* Kübler. After the bloodletting in Poland it had been transferred to the Eifel, the Rhine, and the Ahr Valley to rest and train replacements, spending the winter of 1939-40 there. In the spring of 1940 it began preparations for the attack on France. From its area of concentration in the hilly Eifel Region the founding division of the mountain corps crossed the Meuse, and soon afterward reached the Oise Canal, near Coucy-le-Château, where the mountain infantry, pioneers, and artillery experienced tough positional warfare. The cost was high. Out of misplaced elitism, Kübler refused armored support for his hard-pressed troops. As a result, after a march of 350 kilometers, mainly over flat terrain, his troops were worn out when the time came for the drive into the heart of France. The German Western Army resumed its attack on 5 June 1940. On the evening of the following day, after a series of tough battles, the leading elements of the *1. Gebirgs-Division* crossed the Aisne River 25 kilometers south of the Oise Canal. French resistance soon collapsed, and on 8 June the enemy positions were breached. Ignoring the division's lagging neighbors, Kübler and his "Flower Devils" stormed southwards. They crossed the Ourcq and then, on Kübler's initiative, the Marne, site of the famous First World War battle. The mountain troops continued their victorious advance through Gien to Cher. There the Edelweis Division turned toward Lyon, in the rear of the French alpine front. The division had taken 11,000 prisoners and much booty.

Following the German-French armistice signed at Compiègne, the *1. Gebirgs-Division* was transferred

89

to the Jura region. For a long time it performed guard duties on the demarcation line (the border between occupied and unoccupied France). It appeared that the division's war was over. Soon afterwards, however, it was transferred to the Channel Coast to prepare for "Operation Sea Lion," and then to Besancon for "Operation Feliz." The first operation was an invasion of England, the second an assault on the fortress of Gibraltar in the Mediterranean. The decision to employ the "First" in these operations, neither of which took place, was a reflection of the high regard in which the division was held by the high commands of the *Wehrmacht* and Army.

After the conclusion of the Western Campaign *General* Kübler assumed command of the new *XXXXIX. Gebirgs-Armeekorps* formed in the Besancon area. *General* Lanz was placed in command of the *1. Gebirgs-Division*, which had to release its veteran *Gebirgs-Jäger-Regiment 100* and elements of *Gebirgs-Artillerie-Regiment 79* to form part of the establishment of the new *5. Gebirgs-Division*. Toward the end of the fighting in France the *6. Gebirgs-Division*, which had been formed under *General* Schörner, who led the division with an iron hand, was committed on the Upper Rhine front as part of Army Group South (also Army Group C, Ritter von Leeb). It received its baptism of fire in piercing the Maginot Line on the left bank of the Rhine and fighting in the Vosges and at St. Dié. On 20 June Hartmannswelerkopf, scene of heavy fighting in the First World War, returned to German hands. Two days later the French forces in Alsace-Lorraine laid down their weapons.

It remains to be added that on 10 June 1940, contrary to the wishes of the German command, Mussolini's forces crossed the Italian-French border in an attempt to take a piece of the "victory pie." This marked Italy's entry into the war as an active participant; cause for her ally Germany to rejoice, one would think, but in the beginning that was not the case.

Assembly area for the Western Campaign in the Eifel Mountains.

General der Gebirgstruppe *Ludwig Kübler at the head of his* **1. Gebirgs-***Division.*

91

Mountain infantry cross the French border.

"Open fire!" Aiming over open sights, the artillery in action, probably a 100-mm Kanone 18.

Mountain infantry use an improvised push-cart to transport weapons and equipment as they advance hundreds of kilometers on foot.

Knocked-out bunker in the Maginot Line.

This bunker embrasure displays evidence of a heavy bombardment.

Where is the enemy? The division command makes an on-the-spot assessment of the rapidly-changing situation during the advance into the heart of France.

94

A battalion headquarters staff assesses the situation in a green meadow.

Members of a mountain reconnaissance battalion's bicycle troop immediately display a keen interest in a knocked-out French tank.

95

Right: This Renault B1 tank was put out of action by German forces.

Another abandoned B1. This French heavy tank was armed with a 47-mm cannon mounted in a revolving turret and a 75-mm weapon in the forward hull. In May 1940 the French Army had about 3,000 armored vehicles, including approximately 380 B1s, significantly more than the Wehrmacht could field. Unlike the Germans, however, the French did not employ their tanks in concentration, instead committing them singly or in small groups to support the infantry.

A horse-drawn wagon belonging to a mountain infantry unit passes a knocked-out B1. The bulk of the German units had to depend on horse-drawn vehicles. Even later in the war, the idea of an essentially motorized Wehrmacht was largely wishful thinking.

Even Hitler, who possessed an astonishing knowledge of details, was interested in French armored technology. In terms of quality and firepower, French tanks were equal to those of the Wehrmacht.

Makeshift crossing over a small stream.

June 1940: mountain infantry cross the Aisne in inflatable rafts. The mule swam alongside the raft, guided by a long lead.

The last section of a pontoon bridge is maneuvered into position.

A column of pack animals crosses a pontoon bridge over the Marne near Château-Thierry.

99

Pioneers bridge a river, providing a temporary replacement for the blown bridge in the background.

Captured French artillery, in this case 155-mm heavy howitzers (Canon de 155 C mle 1917 schneider).

Trail of destruction on the advance roads used by the "Flower Devils."

"Men, horses, and wagons…" This conglomeration of wrecked and abandoned wagons and motor vehicles, civilian and military, illustrates the folly of war.

The **1.** *Gebirgs-Division has reached Lyon.*

Above and following: Mountain troops and horse-drawn vehicles of General Schörner's 6. Gebirgs-Division on the advance on the Upper Rhine front near Maisons du Bois.

French equipment captured by the 6. Gebirgs-Division.

French colonial troops captured by a German mountain infantry unit.

105

After capture, this Senegalese soldier was given a cigarette by German mountain troops. He does not appear to be unhappy about his fate.

General der Gebirgstruppe *Kübler on the Atlantic Coast during preparations for "Operation Sea Lion."*

106

Mountain infantry during a landing exercise on the Channel Coast.

For most mountain troops this was the first time in their lives that they had swum in the Atlantic Ocean.

107

General *Julius Ringel decorates members of his* **5. Gebirgs-Division** *after the conquest of Crete.*

The Balkans Campaign 1941

Mussolini wanted a Mediterranean empire for Italy to rival the Roman Empire. For this reason, in 1940 he attacked Greece. This unprovoked attack was in no way in keeping with the desires or plans of the German command. Even worse: though superior in numbers and materiel, the Italians were unable to overcome the Greeks, who were supported by Great Britain. In the winter of 1940-41 the victorious Greeks even invaded Italian-held Albania. After a coup in Yugoslavia overthrew a government friendly to Germany, Hitler saw himself forced to invade and occupy both Greece and Yugoslavia, something he originally had no intention of doing.

The *1., 4., 5.*, and *6. Gebirgs-Division* all took part in the campaign, as well as the *XVIII.* and *XXXXIX. Gebirgs-Armeekorps.*

The *1. Gebirgs-Division* under *General* Lanz, reduced to two infantry regiments after the departure of its third mountain infantry regiment, was attached to Kübler's *XXXXIX. Gebirgs-Armeekorps.* In cold, wet spring weather the division pierced the Yugoslavian fortifications on the Misbach and the raging Drau. In a headlong charge reminiscent of the advance on Lvov it reached Cilli, more than 50 kilometers from the frontier, and sent its veteran motorized *Vorausabteilung Lang* (advance detachment) south to the Croatian capital of Agram (Zagreb) and Bihaç in Bosnia.

In March-April other German units, including the newly-formed *4. Gebirgs-Division* under *General* Eglseer, attacked Yugoslavia from Bulgaria, crossing the icy high ground in the Slatina-Pirot area. On 9 April Serbia was invaded north of Nisch. There "Gentian Division" fought a number of battles in the mountains. After a march of more than 350 kilometers, the Fourth's Yugoslavian campaign came to an end on 14 April. The multi-ethnic state was defeated in less than two weeks, partly because dissatisfied Slovenia and catholic Croatia both had long-standing differences with the radical Orthodox Serbs and were not inclined to resist. On 10 April 1941 Croatia declared itself an independent state, fulfilling a long-standing Croatian desire.

The invasion of Greece was carried out by the *12. Armee* under *Generalfeldmarschall* Wilhelm List. *General* Franze Böhme commanded the *XVIII. Gebirgs-Armeekorps*, to which were attached *General* Ringel's *5. Gebirgs-Division* and *General* Schörner's *6. Gebirgs-Division*. In the north, mountain troops breached the heavily-fortified Metaxas Line in two days. By 27 April all of mainland Greece had been occupied by German troops. The *5. Gebirgs-Division*'s breakthrough at the Rupl Pass along the Struma, and its advance over the snow-capped peaks of the Rhodopen, and the *6. Gebirgs-Division*'s crossing of the snowy Belasca Mountains west of the deep Struma valley leading to Salonika were the outstanding mountain operations of the campaign.

At Mount Olympus, where the German war flag was soon raised, and the historic battlefield of Thermopylae, the British forces sent to bolster the Greeks were defeated and forced to leave the Greek mainland. The way was thus open to the Greek capital. The "Sixth" entered Athens on 27 April 1941 after three weeks of fighting and a march of 600 kilometers. Schörner was hailed as the "Victor of Athens." He and 10 other soldiers of the *6. Gebirgs-Division* were awarded the Knight's Cross of the Iron Cross.

The campaign in the Balkans was not yet over, however, for the Greek island of Crete was still firmly entrenched with British and New Zealand troops. On 19 May, therefore, final preparations were made for "Operation Mercury," the invasion of the Mediterranean island. Transport aircraft and ships stood ready to transport airborne and mountain troops to Crete, a risky venture.

On 20 May 1941 German paratroopers were dropped on airfields on the rocky island, whose highest peaks reach 2 400 meters. The next day mountain infantry of the *5. Gebirgs-Division* followed to reinforce the paratroopers. Transported partly in Greek fishing boats and partly by air, the division was dubbed the "*Luftlande-Marine-Division*" (airborne navy division). As soon as the Ju 52s landed near Maleme the mountain troops joined the fierce fighting. Finally, in the last third of May, Ringel's "Flower Devils," together with units of the *6. Gebirgs-Division*, and of course the parachute troops, took the mountainous island of the Minotaur in blistering heat. On the beach at Skafia, *Gebirgs-Jäger Regiment 100* took no less than 10,000 British, Australian, New Zealand, and Greek prisoners from every service. On 31 May *Gebirgs-Jäger Regiment 85*, with several light mountain guns, reached Heraklion and took up quarters in the area around the city. From June until October the mountain troops served as an occupation force, guarded prisoners, and rooted out remnants of the British forces and Greek partisans. *General* Ringel and 11 members of his "Chamois Division" were awarded the Knight's Cross for their actions. Later the mountain and parachute troops who had taken part in "Operation Mercury" were presented the "Crete" armband, created on 16 October 1942.

The Balkans Campaign lasted just a few weeks. There were two main reasons for this: first, with its mountain units and Blitzkrieg strategy, the *Wehrmacht* was far superior to the Yugoslavian and Greek armies, the latter badly battered from its war with the Italians (leaving out the British forces, which German troops met on the first day of the campaign). Second, cooperation between the air force and army, as well as parachute and mountain troops, was exemplary.

The German command failed to take advantage of Crete—a natural aircraft carrier—as a springboard to North Africa to seize Egypt and the Suez Canal, the lifeline of the British Empire, just as it failed to take Gibraltar due to the reluctance of the Spanish to take part.

Mountain artillerymen of the **1. Gebirgs-Division** *in Klagenfurt prior to the start of the Balkans campaign.*

The troops were transported to the assembly areas by rail.

Mountain infantry use a brief stop to wash up and brush their teeth.

General *Hubert Lanz, commander of the* **1. Gebirgs-Division,** *issues orders to the officers of his advance detachment in the border region.*

Mountain pioneers with cleared Serbian anti-tank mines.

General *Lanz (right) and his two regimental command-ers observe the progress of the attack.*

General *Karl Eglseer issues orders to officers of his* **4.** Gebirgs-Division.

The "Gentian Division" *(4. Gebirgs-Division) crosses a makeshift bridge over the Danube near Belgrade.*

Unloading a ferry in Serbia.

Bicycle troops of a reconnaissance battalion work their way through the Serbian mud.

115

Mountain troops share their rations with hungry Serbian children.

Standing on a Panzer IV, General *Karl Eglseer addresses men of his* **4. Gebirgs-Division.**

After the campaign, General *Eglseer presents the Iron Cross to mountain troops who distinguished themselves in action.*

The 6. Gebirgs-Division crosses the snowy Petrohan Pass in Bulgaria, an ally of Germany. In the photograph the ever popular "Goulash Cannon" (field kitchen).

117

German troops reach the Greek border.

Assault on Istibei, a fortified hill in the Greek Metaxas Line, on 6 April 1941. In this photo, taken during the preparatory bombardment, artillery shells may be seen bursting on the hill.

Mountain infantry on the advance in Greece.

Mountain infantry in position on the Kalmbak, facing the Struma Valley.

Encounter with an assault gun battery in Greece.

Pack animal echelon near Gonos, south of Mount Olympus.

On the heels of the Greeks. The soldier on the right of the photo is using a rangefinder.

121

Captured Greek soldiers. Their attitude toward the defeated was extremely chivalrous. Soldiers of the defeated Epirus Army were even allowed to take their sidearms with them into captivity.

Opposite: General *Ferdinand Schörner, the "Victor of Athens," touring the Acropolis after the fall of Athens. He is accompanied by German and Italian officers.*

On approach to the Greek island of Crete in the Mediterranean.

Mountain infantry in tropical uniforms prepare to board a Ju 52 for transport to Crete.

Above: Mountain anti-tank gunners with their 37-mm anti-tank gun after landing at Maleme. Wrecked transports are stark reminders of the fierce battle for the vital airfield, which was taken by German parachute troops.

Right: "And so many fell...." A paratrooper's grave on Crete.

British and New Zealand troops march through
Rethymnon on their way to a POW camp.

The soldiers removed every piece of unnecessary clothing in the unbearable heat, even their tropical uniforms. These infantrymen are leading a Cretan donkey instead of the usual pack mule.

General der Gebirgstruppe *Julius Ringel addresses men of his "Gentian Division" after the fall of Crete.*

On the climb—German mountain infantry in the Caucasus, 1942. In the background snow-capped peaks reaching to four- and five-thousand meters.

The Russian Campaign
1941-1942/43

By the end of May 1941 the *1. Gebirgs-Division* had assembled in northern Slovakia, in the Presov area. There, between the wooded Carpathians and the High Tatra, at the end of May *General* Lanz received the first warning orders for "Operation Barbarossa." The *Wehrmacht* would be moving east at the beginning of June. For reasons of secrecy, most movements into the assembly areas took place at night. By 20 June the regiments and battalions had moved into their jumping-off and firing positions along the demarcation line between German and Soviet territory, which ran across Poland. Every mountain soldier had the feeling that he was on the threshold of a tremendous event that would surely impact on world history. On the day of the German attack, 22 June 1941, its forces were grouped from East Prussia to Romania, as follows:

Three German army groups faced three similar Soviet formations (fronts). In the north *Generalfeldmarschall* Ritter von Leeb's Army Group North, with 26 divisions, faced Marshal Voroshilov's Baltic Front, with 33 divisions and 6 motorized brigades and divisions. The 48 divisions of Army Group Center under *Generalfeldmarschall* von Bock faced Marshal Timoshenko's Western Front with 46 divisions and 9 motorized brigades and divisions. In the south, *Generalfeldmarschall* von Rundstedt's Army Group South, with 41 German and 16 Romanian divisions, came up against Marshal Budyonny's Southwest Front, with 77 divisions and 14 motorized brigades and divisions.

On 22 June 1941 the German Eastern Army and the allied forces of Hungary, Romania, and Bulgaria, plus Slovakian and Italian units, moved out of its assembly areas and crossed the Soviet border. Part of Army Group South, the *XXXXIX. Gebirgs-Armeekorps* with the *1.* and *4. Gebirgs-Division*, was committed in the direction of Lvov.

After fierce border fighting the mountain soldiers took the Galician capital for the second time. At the end of July they pierced the Stalin Line, then achieved victory at Vinnitsa. After seemingly endless forced marches through the expanses of the Ukraine, at the beginning of August the mountain troops arrived in the Uman area. There, with his two mountain divisions, the *97. leichte Infanterie-Division*, and other formations, *General* Kübler fought the corps battle of Podviskoye, which went into the history books as the Battle of Uman, a classic battle of encirclement. Much of the Soviet 6th and 12th Armies was destroyed. Approximately 60,000 Red Army troops, including the two army commanders, were captured, along with about 100 guns and 50 tanks.

There was no time to rest, however. The advance by the mountain units continued—across the mighty Dniepr, over which the army and mountain pioneers threw a 480-meter pontoon bridge on the night of 8-9 September 1941—and into the Nogay Steppe, an area without landmarks. After heavy fighting at the anti-tank ditches near Timoshevka, the men wearing the edelweiss reached Stalino and the Mius and Samara Rivers. Inadequately clothed and ill-equipped to meet the cold, they and the Italian "Celere" Division prepared to endure their first Russian winter, which was to prove harsh even by Russian standards. There was bitter cold, and fighting flared up in late 1941-early 1942; however, the morale of the mountain troops was not shaken.

At this point less us draw an interim balance. In the first phase of the Russian campaign, which lasted until August 1941, the Soviet armies were driven back along the entire front to a line Leningrad-Smolensk-Kiev-Odessa. In the second offensive phase the entire Donets Basin was taken by September 1941, and in the third, which lasted until the end of November, the attack was carried to the outskirts of Moscow. As a result of the autumn muddy period and the extremely harsh winter that followed, in which the allied forces, with the possible exception of the Finns, were poorly equipped to deal with the extreme cold, Army Group Center suffered severe setbacks. This vital sector of the front faced total collapse, in part because of Hitler's interference. In this tense situation, in December 1941 *General* Kübler assumed command of the *4. Armee* west of Moscow. Four weeks later, however, Hitler dismissed him for failing as commander of an army and sent him home.

The Red Army launched a series of counterattacks that pushed the German units back to a line Taganrog - Orel - Rszhev - Velikiye Luki. The fresh and well-equipped Siberian units failed to destroy Army Group Center, however. The German forces fought desperately to hold the front, suffering heavy losses in men and materiel, and by spring 1942 had overcome the crisis that might have led to the collapse of the entire German eastern front. Even the deep Soviet penetration against Army Group South south of Poltava ended in a German victory, with the *1. Gebirgs-Division* under *General* Lanz playing a significant role in the Battle of Izyum.

In May 1942 the German command was determined to eliminate a dangerous salient extending into the front near Kharkov. Lanz and his mountain troops struck hard. They drove 50 kilometers through Russian units to Barvenkovo, and in the Bereka Valley fought off desperate Soviet attempts to break out. On the night of 24-25 May, however, tens of thousands of Soviet troops rushed the encircling ring on a front of about 100 meters, literally tramping the spring grain into the ground. Losses on both sides were enormous. The founding division of the German mountain troops lost no less than 431 killed and 1,300 wounded.

In the early summer of 1942 the *Wehrmacht*, together with Italian, Romanian, Hungarian, and Slovakian units, launched its offensive in the southern sector. Attacking from the Don Bend, a northern attack force was to drive east to the bend in the Volga at Stalingrad, while a southern force advanced south toward the oil regions of Maykop and Grozny (a name with which many readers may be familiar from the Russian struggle against the Chechens several years ago), which equated to an assault on the Caucasus. Hitler declared that "The Russian is at the end of his strength." The Supreme Commander's decision to conquer the enemy's industrial and oil-producing regions was based on military-economic considerations. He believed that in this way he could force the decision. His main argument was "No army can survive defeats such as the Russian Army has suffered." So at the end of July 1942 Army Group A under *Generalfeldmarschall* List advanced south from bridgeheads on the lower Don. On the right was the *17. Armee* (*V. Armeekorps*, *XXXXIV. Jägerkorps*, and *XXXXIX. Gebirgs-Armeekorps*), in the center the *1. Panzer-Armee* (*XXX.* and *XXXX. Panzer-Armeekorps*), and on the left the *4. Panzer-Armee*. For operations in the high mountains of the Caucasus, however, the German command had just three mountain divisions: the *1.* and *4. Gebirgs-Division*, and the Romanian 1st Mountain Division. The Italian *Alpini* divisions, which followed

130

far behind in the second line, saw no action in the Caucasus, as they were soon diverted in the direction of the Volga.

In spite of this, the four divisions of the *XXXXIX. Gebirgs-Armeekorps* under *General* Rudolf Konrad forced a crossing of the Don near Rostov, where the river was widest, kicking open the door to the Caucasus. Beginning on 12 August, the *1.* and *4. Gebirgs-Division* took the high passes of the Caucasus between Mount Elbrus and the Adsapsch Pass. This marked the true beginning of the struggle for this huge mountain massif between Europe and Asia. The *XXXXIX. Gebirgs-Armeekorps* was sent over the high passes of the Western Caucasus toward Suchum. On 25 August the corps' *4. Gebirgs-Division* captured the Adsapsch and Sancharo Passes (2700 m). Then, on 28 August, it took the Atschavischar Pass, 20 km south of the high crest, and just one day's march from the Black Sea coast.

On 17 August the *1. Gebirgs-Division* had stormed the important Kluchor Pass (2 813 m), securing the corps' left flank at the Elbrus passes. The "Edelweis Division" was unable to break out of the high mountains near Klitsch, however, as strong enemy forces drove into its right flank through the Maruchskoj Pass (2790 m). While the assault on the passes continued on a broad front in the sectors of the *1.* and *4. Gebirgs-Division*, a team of 19 men from the two divisions, all with mountain-climbing experience, scaled the highest peak in the Caucasus. On 21 August 1942 they raised the Reich war flag atop Mount Elbrus (5633 meters).

In the period from 28 August to 5 September 1942, the *1. Gebirgs-Division* succeeded in destroying the enemy forces (roughly brigade strength) advancing through the Maruchskoj Pass. Battle Group Eisgruber achieved this feat by skillfully outflanking the enemy in difficult terrains at elevations of between 3000 and 4000 meters. Elsewhere, however, the situation was worsening. The *XXXXIV. Jägerkorps*' attack through the Caucasus forests toward Tuapse had ground to a standstill. The absence of the Alpini, and logistical difficulties caused by the inadequate road network in the Caucasus, forced Army Group A to halt its advance into the High Caucasus.

The Supreme Command now attempted to get the stalled attack on Tuapse moving again, committing three army corps, including the regrouped *XXXXIX. Gebirgs-Armeekorps*. The high mountain front was to be held while this assault went ahead. The "Lanz Division," formed from units drawn from the *1.* and *4.*

Gebirgs-Division, was to spearhead the drive through the wooded Pontian Caucasus. While the division did succeed in taking the 1036-meter-high Semashko at great cost, the onset of the autumn rains and heavy casualties compelled the German leadership to suspend this operation just short of its objective.

The catastrophe at Stalingrad and the general over-extension of human and materiel resources now forced Germany and its allies onto the retreat. At the turn of the year, therefore, the *XXXXIX. Gebirgs-Armeekorps*, with its two divisions, began a withdrawal on a front of 400 kilometers. Lasting three months, the retreat saw the corps withdraw from the Caucasus to the Kuban bridgehead.

A great shift in military fortunes on the Eastern Front began at the end of 1942-beginning of 1943. First, in late November 1942 the Soviets had broken through positions held by the Italians and Romanians, and then encircled *Generaloberst* Paulus' *6. Armee* with approximately 220,000 men. At the beginning of 1943 the German-Romanian defense lines on the Don were overrun, and the Soviets advanced across the Donets.

But let us flash back to the start of 1942, when German mountain troops were in action against the Soviets with both Army Groups South and North. Despite massive Russian counterattacks, the front before Leningrad, on the Volkhov, and Lake Ilmen were held until spring 1942. The battles fought by *General* Ringel's *5. Gebirgs-Division*, which was later given the fitting nickname of "Swamp-Jäger Division," and *General* Martinek's *7. Gebirgs-Division*, which served in the fire-brigade role on the roads before Leningrad and at Lake Ilmen, were among the hardest and costliest ever fought by German mountain troops.

After the fall of Kiev, the *99. leichte Infanterie-Division* had been pulled out of the line and sent to Grafenwöhr to be reorganized as the *7. Gebirgs-Division*. It was to have been shipped to Finland in January 1942, however, this plan was frustrated when the Baltic froze over. In February, therefore, elements of the new division, principally mountain infantry and artillery, were sent to "Assault Group Seidlitz," whose mission was to attack from Staraya Russa and break through to the *II. Armeekorps* encircled at Demyansk. The mountain troops achieved their mission in mid-April after fierce fighting in deep snow and swamp water. Losses were correspondingly high—822 killed, 52 missing, and 2,641 wounded in six weeks.

At the beginning of 1942 the *5. Gebirgs-Division* was transferred from sun-baked Crete to the Salzburg area for a brief period of rest and reorganization, after which it was sent to the Volkhov - Leningrad area. There it fought all over the northern front, at Leningrad, Neva, Mga and Karbusel, Sinyavino, the Kirishi bridgehead, Volkhov, and Lake Ladoga. It fought in the swamps and primeval forests for almost two years until, at the urging of *General* Ringel, it was transferred to the mountainous Italian Theater.

After the costly fighting at the Liza, the *3. Gebirgs-Division* under *General* Kreysing returned to Germany to rest and reequip. In the summer of 1942 it arrived in Army Group North's sector. There it helped repulse a major Soviet offensive, whose objective was the relief of Leningrad. As "Battle Group Klatt," elements of the division were later moved into the Velikiye Luki - Novo Sokolniki area to help prevent a Soviet breakthrough.

By the end of 1942 the fierce fighting cost the battle group casualties of more than 2,000 wounded and 785 killed and missing. There was no letup, however, for the Eastern Front was ablaze from end to end. The "Third" was thrown into the witch's cauldron of Millerovo, where as "Battle Group Kreysing" it was quickly encircled by powerful forces of the Red Army.

Mountain Divisions in the East

The following mountain units were deployed in Russia: the *1. Gebirgs-Division* on the southern front from Lvov through Vinnitsa and the Bug to the Ingulets, during the battle of encirclement at Uman and Podvisloye, in the Nogay Steppe, then through Stalino to the Mius, during the battle of Kharkov, and finally across the Donets and Don to the Caucasus, and the subsequent retreat to the Kuban bridgehead.

The *3. Gebirgs-Division* in the northern sector on Lake Ladoga and at Velikiye Luki, as well as on the southern front at Millerovo, in the Donets Basin, in Nikopol, and the long retreat from the Dniepr across the Bug to the Dnestr.

The *4. Gebirgs-Division* fought mainly side by side with the *1. Gebirgs-Division* during the advance. In 1942 it marched into the Caucasus, and in 1943-44 fought its way back across the Crimea and southern Russia to the northern Carpathians.

The *5. Gebirgs-Division* and the *7. Gebirgs-Division* were primarily deployed in the northern sector at Leningrad and on the Volkhov River.

132

Mountain infantryman with a captured Red Army regimental banner. It bears the slogan of the Communist world revolution: "Proletarians of every nation unite!"

General *Land and* **Oberstleutnant** *Hörl of the* **1.** *Gebirgs-Division study a map.*

Horse-drawn vehicles of the **1. Gebirgs-***Division during the advance on Lvov. In the foreground is a kleiner Feldwagen Hf 3 (small field wagon).*

Troops pass a "big stick." Even for veteran mountain infantrymen the Russian 152-mm heavy field howitzer was an uncommon sight.

*A captured artillery piece. The heavy machine-gun platoon of the **I. Batallion** of Gebirgs-Jäger Regiment 98 was obviously faster than the Soviet artillery.*

Wrecked Soviet tank near Lvov. It is a Type 26 A with twin machine-gun turrets.

*Weighing 43.5 tons with armor up to 75 mm thick, in the summer of 1941 the KV I tank was a tough opponent for the German anti-tank units. This one met its fate on the advance road used by the **1.** and **4. Gebirgs-Division**.*

The appearance of the T 34 in July 1941 came as an unpleasant surprise to the Wehrmacht. Overnight it rendered the standard armament of German tanks and anti-tank units ineffective. Tank expert Walter J. Spielberger characterized this battle tank, which was capable of speeds up to 54 kph and armed with a 76.2-mm gun, as "a perfect symbiosis of the elements mobility, protection, and firepower." As the standard anti-tank weapons proved ineffective against the T 34, many were put out of action by daring attackers armed with hand grenade bundles or by direct artillery fire.

Above: Standing by an open grave, General Lanz bids farewell to 12 mountain infantry killed near Glescyce.

Right: **General der Gebirgstruppe** *Ludwig* **Kübler** *(right) as commanding general of the* **XXXXIX. Gebirgs-Armeekorps,** *and the commanding officer of the* **1. Gebirgs-Division,** *Hubert Lanz, study a map.*

"Where is Guderian with his tanks?" With enemy units approaching, the spearhead awaits urgently-needed support.

Oxcarts commandeered from Russian farmers are used to transport wounded Soviet soldiers.

*Above: The **III.** Batallion of **Gebirgs-Jäger** Regiment 91 during the crossing of the Dniepr. Below: Watering horses at a draw-well.*

This photograph says more than words about road conditions in Russia at the start of the muddy period. When all motorized transport failed, horse-drawn, or in this case mule-drawn, transport continued to function even in the most adverse road and weather conditions.

Horses and vehicle stuck in the snow in the Mius-Samara position. Men and animals performed feats during the winter of 1941-42, the worst in 250 years, so unimaginable that words cannot adequately describe them. Lacking winter clothing and equipment, without rations or shelter, and with no motorized transport, the German troops faced fresh, well-equipped Siberian divisions. Nevertheless, the front held. After the war the British General Fuller wrote: "What the German soldier, totally unprepared for a winter campaign, accomplished, what he did in terms of endurance, represents one of the greatest acts of heroism in recorded military history."

140

Spring in the former winter position on the Samara, 1942.

The battlefield near Kharkov, 1942.

The beginning of the spring offensive in the southern sector of the Eastern Front, 1942.

Approximately 10,000 Red Army soldiers were taken prisoner.

Mountain infantry on the advance in the Caucasus.

143

First encounter with Soviets of Asiatic and Caucasian origin. Many of the latter went over to the German side.

August 1942: mountain anti-tank troops in the Caucasus.

Pack animal column in the High Caucasus.

A patrol gets ready. The man on the right is carrying a Russian PPSh 41 machine-pistol, a weapon prized by German troops.

A mountain artillery pack column approaches the apex of a mountain pass.

The faithful mule climbing a steep slope.

147

Above: Outpost in the rock and ice. Below: On the way to the peak of Mount Elbrus. On 21 August 1942 soldiers of a hand-picked Kapitän drawn from the 1. and 4. Gebirgs-Division raised the German flag and the Edelweis pennant atop Elbrus, the highest peak in the Caucasus (5 633 meters).

The German mountain infantry had marched hundreds of kilometers and taken positions and passes thought to be invulnerable, but were unable to cross the "last few meters" to the coast. Soviet resistance had become too strong, the German supply lines too extended, and the available forces inadequate. Moving down from the high mountain passes.

In the hell of the forested Caucasus, Christmas Eve 1942. The peaceful impression made by this photograph is deceiving. Countless mountain troops died of hunger and exhaustion, or were killed by the revived Soviets.

In the northern sector of the Eastern Front. A troop train steams toward Leningrad.

Above: The vastness of the land, crossed by mighty rivers, repeatedly gave the enemy opportunities to withdraw.

Intersection with typical road signs.

151

Mountain pioneers on the Neva.

Facing page and above: constructing positions and billets.

*On the Volkhov. Although he looks like a dispatch rider, this is in fact an **Oberleutnant** on a motorcycle-sidecar combination.*

Vehicles on a raised roadway through the marshy terrain along the Volkhov River.

Most roads looked like this, however.

An armored troop carrier in the muddy slop that the German soldiers sarcastically referred to as "Russian asphalt."

Horses collapsed from exhaustion or were killed by enemy fire.

A forest of road signs on the Volkhov Front.

A sign showing the way home—2448 kilometers to Klagenfurt!

Field railway in action—the "Volkhov Express."

The Soviets suffered huge losses in the fierce fighting. Shown here is a wrecked T 34. The inscription on the turret reads "sa rodinu" (for the homeland).

General der Gebirgstruppe *Julius Ringel, commander of the* 5. Gebirgs-Division, *with his "Swamp Troops" at Lake Ladoga. Note the non-regulation salute of the Leutnant reporting to the General. "Papa" Ringel was not one to insist on formalities.*

At the 5. Gebirgs-Division's *command post.*

159

Watering horses on the Volkhov Front.

Cemetery of the **III.** *Batallion of* **Gebirgs-Jäger** *Regiment 206 of the* **7.** **Gebirgs-Divi-**
sion south of Staraya Russa.

Machine-gun position of **Gebirgs-Jäger** *Regiment 91 in the* **Kuban** *bridgehead, September 1943. Regimental commander* **Oberst** *Hörl (right) personally directs fire.*

The Eastern Front in Retreat 1943-1944/45

In spite of the heavy losses suffered by the German Eastern Army during the winter of 1942-43, the *Wehrmacht* High Command planned new attacks for the spring of 1943 in order to seize the initiative from the enemy. While these gained no ground, they did make it possible to parry Soviet operations that began in the summer. Shortly after New Year 1943, *General* Lanz handed the *1. Gebirgs-Division* over to his successor, Ritter von Grabenhofen. After defensive fighting on the left wing of the Kuban bridgehead, the founding division of the mountain corps was suddenly transferred to the Balkans to fight partisans. The only mountain units left in the southern sector of the Eastern Front were Headquarters, XXXXIX. *Gebirgs-Armeekorps* and the *4. Gebirgs-Division*. The latter division was commanded by *General* Kress until his death in action at the Myshako, and from August 1943 by *General* Braun. It fought several fierce battles at the Gentian Division's fateful mountain, where it suffered casualties of 898 killed and wounded in a single day's fighting, and opposed the major Soviet landing at Novorossisk.

In autumn 1943 the German front in the east was pulled back to the Mariupol - Dniepr - Vitebsk defense line. This made it necessary for the Kuban bridgehead to be evacuated by the *17. Armee*, together with the *V. Armeekorps*, the *XXXXIV. Jägerkorps*, and the *XXXXIX. Gebirgs-Armeekorps. General* Konrad was placed in command of the final movement. In a withdrawal operation lasting three weeks, the last six divisions abandoned the front along the lagoons and were transported across the Strait of Kerch to the Crimean Peninsula. The very last unit to leave the bridgehead was *Gebirgs-Jäger Regiment 13* of the *4. Gebirgs-Division*.

Every Soviet attempt to strike the rear of the *XXXXIX. Gebirgs-Armeekorps* from land or sea was defeated. More impressive is the fact that neither weapons nor vehicles were lost in this unique evacuation.

Those who fought in the Kuban were later awarded the Kuban Shield, created on 20 September 1943.

The *XXXXIX. Gebirgs-Armeekorps* was now in command of most of the Crimea, and immediately set about bolstering the fortifications of the marine fortress of Sevastopol, which had been taken in 1942 (then the largest fortress in the world). The *Gebirgs-Armeekorps* and its attached units also began constructing three major defense lines at equal intervals between the Sivash and Sevastopol to repel any invasion of the peninsula from the north. All of these measures later helped make it possible for the front to be held, at least for a time, with relatively minor forces.

In October 1943 the *4. Gebirgs-Division* was attached to the newly-formed *6. Armee*. Soon, however, the army was forced to withdraw toward Odessa and Nikopol in the face of Soviet pressure.

The decisive battle for the Crimea began on 8 April 1944, after Hitler categorically refused a planned evacuation of the peninsula, which would have saved the German and Romanian units there for subsequent operations. His fear that the surrender of the Crimea might lead the Turks to declare war on Germany prevented the Supreme Commander from making a decision that made sense militarily. As a result, the Crimea was the scene of further unnecessary, costly fighting. Sevastopol held out for a month before it fell.

Let us flash back to events on the Eastern Front one year earlier: 1943 saw the *3. Gebirgs-Division* engaged in interrupted defensive fighting between the Sea of Azov and the Donets. Battle Group Kreysing was encircled at Millerovo, but the "Flower Devils" refused to surrender to the Soviets. Instead, in one final desperate act, on 14 January they broke through the ring of enemy forces and fought their way to the Donets Basin, a distance of approximately 100 kilometers. At the end of February the division fought a successful action near Voroshilovgrad. By mid-August the front became frozen in positional warfare.

In August *General* Kreysing handed the *3. Gebirgs-Division* over to *General* Picker, who in turned handed it over to *General* Wittmann in October. From the end of October until February 1944 the division fought costly defensive battles at Redkina, west of Kubyshevo and east of Novo Laspa. It also saw action in the "Lizard" and "Wotan" positions in the Nikopol bridgehead, where the Third's combat strength at times was only 1,500 men. After 100 days, heavy enemy pressure forced the division to evacuate the bridgehead

at the cost of much of its equipment. After the evacuation of Nikopol, the *3. Gebirgs-Division* took part in fierce winter battles with the new *6. Armee*, destroying more than 450 Soviet tanks. It subsequently withdrew across the Ingulets, Igul, and Bug Rivers, finally seeing action in the Carpathian Mountains in June 1944. Following the loss of Romania and the collapse of Army Group South Ukraine, the division under *General* Klatt conducted a fighting withdrawal, reaching the Theiss in November 1944.

After its costly actions near Melitopol and seven weeks of fighting in the Kherson bridgehead, at the turn of the year 1943-44 the *4. Gebirgs-Division* was hastily moved by train via Odessa to Vinnitsa. There it conducted offensive and defensive operations in meeting a massive Soviet advance. After numerous defensive actions between Uman and Kirovograd, at the beginning of March 1944 it managed to fight its way across the Bug to the Dnestr in spite of massive enemy pressure.

After a severe crisis, at the very last minute the Gentian Division succeeded in halting attempts by the Soviets to break through between Grigoriopol and Koshnitsa on the Dnestr. The affair at Koshnitsa was still weighing heavily on the division when *General* Breith assumed command. At the end of July the "Fourth" was transferred to the northern Carpathians. Between 6 and 23 August, fighting in difficult forest terrain, it defeated all Soviet advances at the Tatar Pass and drove the enemy out of the mountains. After the collapse of Romania the Carpathian passes in the east had to be kept open to provide an avenue of retreat for the remnants of the *6. Armee*, indeed until the start of the general retreat in September 1944. Finally, the *4. Gebirgs-Division* on the Theiss and the *3. Gebirgs-Division* were attached to the *XXXXIX. Gebirgs-Armeekorps* under *General* von le Suire. The two veteran divisions now fought their way together through the High Tatra to Upper Silesia, where by summoning all its strength, the *XXXXIX. Gebirgs-Armeekorps* briefly halted the enemy in the area of Troppau and Olmütz. Soviet armored units broke across the north-Czechoslovakian border, however, and the mountain troops were caught in a trap from which there was no escape.

Most of the mountain troops became prisoners of the Soviets, and many were held until after Federal Chancellor Konrad Adenauer's visit to Moscow in 1955.

An **Obergefreiter** *comments on signs on the Nikopol to Balki road.*

Barbed wire (and probably mines beyond it) on the beach of the Sea of Azov, obstacles to an enemy landing.

Aerial supply containers for the Kuban bridgehead.

The original caption reads, "Important conference in the Kuban bridgehead." Two **Obergefreiter** *in conversation with a pipe-smoking* **Oberjäger.**

Foto: Hüster

Two photographs of the Black Sea port of Novorossisk, scene of fierce fighting by the **4. Gebirgs-Division.**

On 6 February 1943 the Soviets attempted a landing in the Bay of Osereika. It was repulsed with heavy losses. In the photograph wrecked landing craft.

A German bunker position, photographed after the failed Soviet landing attempt south of Novorossisk.

170

Generalleutnant *Hermann Kress, commander of the* **4.** **Gebirgs-***Division, in Novorossisk.*

The rain and mud returned, but at least the German army in the east had proper clothing during the second autumn and winter in Russia. It had also learned how to deal with the elements.

As soon as the first snow fell, vehicles were given a coat of white camouflage paint.

"Forward comrades, we must retreat!"

174

It was hoped that anti-tank ditches would halt the Soviets.

The remains of a T 34 whose ammunition detonated, destroying the tank.

General *Ferdinand Schörner (right), commanding general of the* **XXXX. Panzer-Armeekorps,** *discusses the less than rosy situation with* **General Wittmann,** *commander of the* **3. Gebirgs-***Division, in the spring of 1944.*

Pontoon bridge in the Nikopol bridgehead.

Mountain infantry patrol leader during house-to-house fighting in Nikopol.

Mountain infantry in a trench near Nikopol.

179

The terrible face of war—this Red Army soldier was burned to death while trying to abandon his knocked-out tank.

A peaceful scene: mountain infantry in front of a Russian Orthodox church. The atheistic Soviets frequently desecrated churches by using them as cow barns or storage sites.

The battery commander's worry before and during loading: where will I put everything?

181

Officers and a senior NCO of a mountain battery check the 4-meter rangefinder.

Generals, too, are entitled to leave and relaxation: **Generalleutnant** *Julius Braun,* **commander of the 4. Gebirgs-Division,** *in the "Enz" rest and recreation facility in Abrau (summer 1943).*

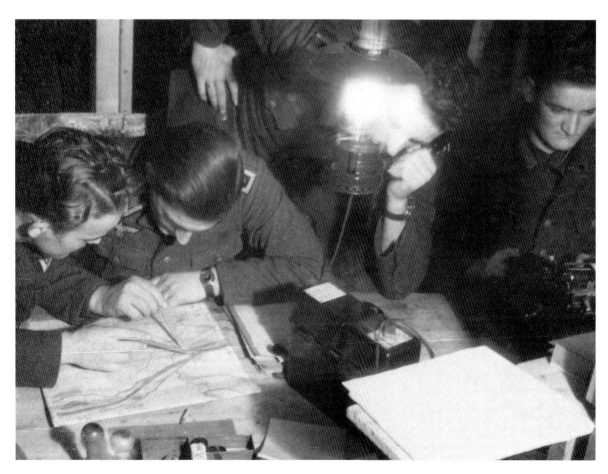

November-December 1943: hectic activity in the Gentian Division's command post in the Kherson bridgehead.

German and Romanian soldiers in conversation with Bessarabian farmers in the market in Kishinev.

185

Generalleutnant *Friedrich Breith, the fourth and last commander of the* **4. Gebirgs-Division**, *with his operations officer, General Staff Major Hans Brandner, in autumn 1944.*

Flooding in the marshy region of Cape Nages Callos.

Slovakian border guards in the Carpathians, autumn 1944.

Adjutants conference, **4. Gebirgs-Division**, *11 January 1945 in the Pelsöc area. The Soviet offensive began the next day.*

On the wintry Polar Sea front. A ski patrol moves out.

The Scandinavian Theater
1941-1945

As preparations were underway from Finland to the Black Sea for the coming invasion of the Soviet Union, from April to June 1941 *Gebirgskorps Norwegen* (renamed *XIX. Gebirgs-Armeekorps* on 10 November 1942) was transferred from Narvik north into the area of Kirkenes. Some elements of the corps were transported by ship, while others made the difficult journey overland. Elements of *Gebirgs-Jäger Regiment 137*, which had distinguished itself in "Operation Buffalo," covered 350 kilometers over the mountainous terrain of northern Norway, where roads were few, as well as the snow-covered tundra of Lapland in temperatures of minus 30 degrees.

On 29 June 1941 *Gebirgskorps Norwegen*, under the command of *General* Dietl, with *General* Schlemmer's 2. *Gebirgs-Division* and *General* Kreysing's 3. *Gebirgs-Division*, attacked across the Titovka River line in the direction of the Liza, meeting ferocious resistance. The corps' ultimate objective was to reach Murmansk, Russia's only ice-free port, and the Murmansk railway, which led into the heart of Russia. The first daily communiqué, which gave some impression of a landscape totally foreign to central Europeans, read:

"At 0000 hours on 29 June 1941, German mountain troops attacked across frozen tundra in the direction of Murmansk under the light of the midnight sun."

As the events of July and September 1941 would show, the attack was doomed to failure. The mountain troops, the majority of them from Ostmark (Austria), launched three assaults at the fateful Liza River, and none achieved the desired success. Even worse: Dietl, the "Hero of Narvik" and Hitler's darling, was the only commanding general on the entire Eastern Front at that time who failed to reach his operational objective—Murmansk and the "Burma Road of the North." The cost for this failure was high: in the period until mid-October, *Gebirgskorps Norwegen* suffered losses of

191

2,610 killed, 9,229 wounded, and 656 missing! This was the first defeat suffered by the *Wehrmacht*, which had so far known only victory, and it came before the turning of the tide at Moscow. Admittedly, the Soviets were significantly superior in numbers and artillery, and the terrain bestowed definite advantages on the defender. However, the German failure was in large part due to a completely inadequate supply and transportation system. The advance on Murmansk came to a halt after a gain of just 60 kilometers. There was no continuous front as such; instead, a system of widely-scattered strongpoints and field guard positions across the hostile tundra to the neck of the Fisher Peninsula on the Polar Sea.

Prior to the severe winter of 1941-42, the bloodied *3. Gebirgs-Division* was relieved by the *6. Gebirgs-Division*, which had arrived by rail and ship from Greece. The ice-covered Baltic made it impossible to transport out all elements of the division, however, and the veteran *Gebirgs-Jäger Regiment 139* remained in the far north and later formed the cadre regiment of "*Divisionsgruppe Kräutler.*" In spite of his failure to take Murmansk, Dietl, ever popular with his troops, was promoted to *Generaloberst* and placed in command of the *Lappland-Armee*, which on 22 June 1942 was renamed *Gebirgs-Armee-Oberkommando 20* (Headquarters, 20th Mountain Army). From that time on it commanded the following sectors and units:

Louhi-Kiestinki Sector:
Headquarters, *XVIII. Gebirgs-Armeekorps* with the *7. Gebirgs-Division* and the *6. SS-Gebirgs-Division "Nord"* in the area between Toposero and Pyavosero, plus "*Divisionsgruppe Kräutler.*"
Kandalaksha-Salla Sector:
Headquarters, *XXXVI. Gebirgs-Armeekorps* with the *163.* and *169. Infanterie-Division*, which were equipped with skis for this unaccustomed role.
Murmansk Sector:
Headquarters, *XIX. Gebirgs-Armeekorps* with the *2.* and *6. Gebirgs-Division* plus "*Divisionsgruppe van der Hoop.*"

Later placed under the command of *Gebirgs-Armee-Oberkommando 20* were five fortress infantry battalions of the *210. Infanterie-Division*, a *Luftwaffe* regiment, and eight navy coastal batteries attached to the naval commander at Kirkenes. These reinforcements were badly needed, for the *20. Gebirgs-Armee's* theater was one of the most isolated, and included a stretch of weakly-defended Polar Sea coastline along which Allied convoys sailed virtually unhindered to Murmansk. As well, the area was probably the most difficult on the entire Eastern Front to supply. The supply services of the most northern mountain army corps faced a most difficult task.

The mountain troops from Austria survived that first polar winter in their primitive stone bunkers, Finnish tents, and igloos, withstanding frigid temperatures, fierce winter storms, meter-deep snow, and isolation. That they did so was due in large part to the toughness of their commander Schörner, the new commanding general of the *Gebirgskorps Norwegen*. When spring finally did come, however, the troops were put to another severe test, for all signs pointed to a major Soviet offensive against the mountain corps' deep southern flank, which was unguarded.

On 26-27 April 1942 units of the Soviet 14th Army launched a major attack on land and across the Polar Sea. The objective of the offensive, which lasted three weeks, was the destruction of the "Flower Devils." The entire front was set ablaze, with murderous fighting on both flanks and in the so-called northern area. On 5 May the mountain troops faced their greatest crisis: after days of heavy fighting a brigade of Soviet marines almost completed their encirclement. All that separated the Germans from complete encirclement was a few hundred meters. Then the forces of nature seized the initiative. A vicious arctic storm lashed both attackers and defenders for 90 hours. *Gebirgskorps-Norwegen* was in danger of being wiped out. Only by mobilizing the last of their resources were the half-frozen men of the *2.* and *6. Gebirgs-Division* able to fight off the powerful enemy assault and withstand the merciless forces of nature. The Soviets lost about 8,000 men in the fighting.

After the failed Lapland campaign of 1941 and the early spring battle in 1942, the fronts on the Polar Sea, in Lapland and in Karelia, became stationary. The *2., 6.,* and *7. Gebirgs-Division, Divisionsgruppe "Kräutler,"* the *6. SS-Gebirgs-Division "Nord,"* and the *163.* and *169. Infanterie-Division* of the *XXXVI. Gebirgs-Armeekorps* (initially under *General* Weisenberger and later *General* Vogel) held the most northern flank of the Eastern Front. For the troops, monotonous picket duty and exhausting patrols alternated with road building, pack duty, and other supply chores.

The mountain troops' positions were west of the Murmansk railway in the deepest primeval forest. The unfamiliar conditions placed a great strain on the mountain troops. The Soviets launched frequent attacks and large-scale patrols and raids, requiring the German commanders and soldiers to maintain a high level of alertness and combat readiness. Several fierce battles were fought on the Kangasvaara and Nyatovaara Rivers. The only offensive action by the German side in 1943 was the so-called "Battle of Bunker Ridge," which the *7. Gebirgs-Division* and units of the *6. SS-Gebirgs-Division "Nord"* fought in the Karelian forests.

In September 1944 Finland was forced to conclude a ceasefire with the USSR. German forces were obliged to leave the country by 15 September, however, this was easier to order than carry out, for the Soviet marshals had it in mind to isolate and destroy the legendary Lapland Army. This did not happen, however.

The withdrawal of German forces from central Finland was dubbed "Operation Birch." The Soviets launched a massive offensive from the direction of Murmansk, but by summoning the last of its strength, the *XIX. Gebirgs-Armeekorps* under *General* Ferdinand Jodl, with the *2.* and *6. Gebirgs-Division*, successfully screened the withdrawal. After Soviet reprisals, the first hostilities between German and Finnish troops took place near Ranua. Fierce rearguard actions then developed near Ylimaa and Taipalo between the *7. Gebirgs-Division* and the Finnish Puruma Brigade, former comrades in arms.

The retreat by the German divisions from Karelia to the Rovaniemi defense position, and from there into the "Battering Ram" position, was extremely difficult. No less arduous, however, was the withdrawal in Lapland and on the Polar Sea, dubbed "Operation Northern Light." The Soviets launched a major offensive on the Polar Sea front on the night of 6-7 October 1944, its objective to inflict a "Stalingrad of the North" on the German mountain troops. But once again the Soviets underestimated the opposition. In a weeks-long fighting retreat from Petsamo to northern Norway, the German mountain troops frustrated every attempt by the Soviets to encircle and destroy them. Both sides suffered enormous losses—from 1 to 31 October alone, German casualties totaled 5,236 officers, NCOs, and men. But the retreat by approximately 200,000 men was a success—and this in the middle of an Arctic winter with ice, just a few hours of light per day, and horrible road conditions. The main route to northern Norway was *Reichsstrasse 50*, a winding road through Kirkenes and Ivalo, interrupted in many places by deep fiords. The retreat owed its success to the iron discipline of the troops and the command skill of *Generaloberst* Lothar Rendulic, who had assumed command of the *20. Gebirgs-Armee* after Dietl's death in a plane crash.

With the exception of the *2. Gebirgs-Division* and the *6. SS-Gebirgs-Division "Nord,"* which were transported back to the Reich, the German mountain troops that withdrew to Norway late in the war remained there, and were later interned by the Allies. The mountain soldiers of the *Wehrmacht* and *Waffen-SS* would see further action in Upper Alsace, and the headquarters of the *XXXVI. Gebirgs-Armeekorps* found new employment in East Prussia. Many of the "Flower Devils" of the *6.*, *7.*, and *10. Gebirgs-Division* captured by the British were transferred to the Soviets and had to endure years of suffering and deprivation in Stalin's camps.

Mountain Units in the Far North

Of the senior command organizations and divisions of the German mountain troops, the following units saw action in the Lapland campaign and in the Finnish theater of war:

Gebirgs-Armee-Oberkommando 20,
Headquarters, *XVIII. Gebirgs-Armeekorps* ,
Headquarters, *XIX. Gebirgs-Armeekorps*,
Headquarters, *XXXVI. Gebirgs-Armeekorps* plus
the *2. Gebirgs-Division* in Norway, Lapland, and the retreat through the Arctic,
the *3. Gebirgs-Division* in Norway and the Polar Sea front,
the *6. Gebirgs-Division* on the Polar Sea front and the fighting withdrawal to Norway,
the *7. Gebirgs-Division* in Karelia and the retreat through Lapland to Norway in autumn 1944,
the *10. Gebirgs-Division*, previously "Divisionsgruppe Kräutler," in Lapland and Norway,
the *6. SS-Gebirgs-Division "Nord"* in Karelia and Lapland.

Pack animal company resting on **Reichstrasse** *50* **from Alta to Kirkenes.**

Supply road on the northern Polar Sea.

The charismatic General Eduard Dietl (right) with a staff officer while surveying terrain in the tundra.

0300 hours on the morning of 21 June 1941. The assembled troops of the **11. Kompanie** *of* Gebirgs-Jäger Regiment *136 are informed of the coming attack on the Soviet Union. The midnight sun on the Norwegian-Finnish border makes night into day.*

Mountain troops enjoy a carefree moment in a comfortable Finnish tent.

The "Triumvirate" of the Polar Sea front on skis: **General** *Eduard Dietl between* **General** *Georg Ritter von Hengl (right) and* **General** *Ferdinand Schörner.*

Hard work for men and animals under Arctic conditions.

Quarters of the mountain artillery on the Polar Sea front, 1941-42. In the photo is **Wachtmeister** *Alfred Bolkart, who provided a number of the photographs in this book.*

The mountain infantry soon came to appreciate the value of dogsleds for the transport of ammunition and rations.

A ski patrol in camouflage smocks make ready for an attack.

A patrol returns.

202

A battalion command post in the Arctic.

Dog sled in action in the hostile Arctic.

Transporting a wounded man on a sleigh.

Above: Sign on "Mountain Infantry Road" in Karelia.

Right: Signpost in the Louhi-Kiestinki sector.

205

Generaloberst *Dietl, Commander-in-Chief of the legendary Lapland Army, presents decorations to his mountain troops.*

Karelian front, 12 July 1944. Operations briefing in front of the "Dietl House" near Kiestinki. **General der Gebirgstruppe** *Karl Eglseer (back to camera) in conversation with* **Hauptmann** *Erler, who fought at Narvik. Wearing the Knight's Cross is* **Oberleutnant** *Matthes of MG-Bataillon 14.*

Mountain infantry in front of their billet in the wintry Karelian forest.

Ski training in Karelia.

207

Members of an anti-tank unit haul a 75-mm Type 36 mountain gun through deep snow. For concealment they are wearing white snow smocks and white-painted helmets.

Patrol from the 6. SS-Gebirgs-Division "Nord" in front of the so-called Gudrun Position.

Situation briefing by the commander of the 6. SS-Gebirgs-Division "Nord," *SS*-Brigadeführer *and* Generalmajor *der* Waffen-SS *Matthias Kleinheisterkamp (wearing mosquito veil).*

*Mountain infantry of the **Waffen-SS** prepare to set out on a long-range patrol, a five-day sortie to the Murmansk railway. Apart from their weapons, which include captured Soviet machine-pistols, they carry only rations and essential equipment.*

Anti-tank gunners of the **6. SS-Gebirgs-Division "Nord"** *and a knocked-out Soviet tanks near Salla.*

Makeshift crossing over a small stream.

An artillery observer observes Soviet attack preparations through a binocular telescope.

A sentry in a trench of the so-called "Battering Ram Position" during the German retreat from Finland. The 98k carbine with the Mauser 98 breech was a reliable weapon, even in the bitter cold.

The fallen of the Polar Sea front were buried in the German military cemetery in Parkkina in northern Finland. In October 1944 a half dozen Soviet tanks desecrated the cemetery, crushing crosses and flattening grave mounds.

"Operation Black": mountain troops of the Waffen-SS pursue the fleeing enemy. Many days they covered 60 to 70 kilometers on foot through difficult terrain, carrying weapons and other burdens.

The War in the Balkans
1943-1945

After the catastrophe of Stalingrad, the Balkan nations allied with Germany and Italy were increasingly drawn toward the Allies. With the first indications that Germany might be defeated, they finally went over to the enemy side. This sent a shock wave through the Balkans, which by tradition was hostile towards Germany.

After distinguishing itself during operations in the Kuban bridgehead, in March 1943 the *1. Gebirgs-Division* was, without warning, transferred to the Balkans. In 1943-44 the division served there as a "fire-brigade," taking part in difficult and psychologically-demanding operations against the numerous partisan bands active in Greece, Albania, and Yugoslavia. Numerous successes were achieved against the partisans, due in large part to the style of guerilla warfare adopted by the mountain troops of the army and the *Waffen-SS*. By and large, the partisans were held in check until shortly before the end of the war.

After the Badoglio coup, the fall of Mussolini, and the defection of Italy, in late summer 1943 the *1. Gebirgs-Division* was called upon to disarm Italian troops. While this caused few problems on the mainland, the retaking of the strategically-important islands of Corfu and Cefalonia in the Ionian Sea was followed by incidents that severely tarnished the edelweiss and the reputation of the German mountain troops. It is claimed, for example, that on Cefalonia approximately 4,000 Italian soldiers were shot as traitors.

At the end of August 1944 the German-friendly government of Marshal Antonescu in Romania fell. The new Sanatescu government ordered the cessation of hostilities against the Red Army and allied itself with the Soviets, bringing down the entire southern part of the German defense front in the east. Within a few weeks the Soviets occupied Walachia and the Ploesti oil fields, vital to the German war effort. German and Hungarian forces attempted to at least hold the Carpathian line, however, this failed under massive Soviet attacks. By the end of October 1944 all of

217

Transylvania was in enemy hands. The Theiss Plain lay open before the Soviet armies. Well-equipped Soviet forces, bolstered by Asiatic units, advanced irresistibly into Yugoslavia. The weak units of the German army, *Waffen-SS*, navy, air force, and rear-echelon troops, which varied widely in their composition, were forced into difficult and hopeless situations in the mountainous, partisan-infested terrain.

Between 8 and 30 September 1944 the units of the *1. Gebirgs-Division* fought fierce defensive battles between Vlasotine and Zajecar on the Bulgarian-Yugoslavian border. On 30 September an advance by Russian armored forces split the division into three parts: the main group under von Stettner; a battle group commanded by Groth; and the quartermaster section. Caught in a hopeless situation, the "First" was pulled back toward the Morava from 1 to 14 October, resulting in bitter fighting. It then passed through Pozarevac into the area south of Belgrade. On 17 October another group of forces was in retreat west toward Milanovac. When the situation came to a head in the southeast of Belgrade, the *1. Gebirgs-Division* and its commanding officer found themselves facing disaster at the gates of the Yugoslavian capital. Since 5 October strong Soviet forces had been on the north bank of the Danube. Armored units driving toward Belgrade split the von Stettner and Groth groups on the Morava north of Lapovo, while Tito's partisan units destroyed bridges, roads, and other transportation targets behind the front.

Based on available information, on 17 October the division commander abandoned his initial intention of breaking through to the "Rome of the Orthodox Serbs" and decided instead to break out to the west. But at what a cost! Only a few elements of this veteran mountain division, which had distinguished itself on so many battlefronts, succeeded in breaking through to the west, to the Drina. Approximately 5,000 men were left in the Belgrade pocket, including *General* Ritter von Stettner.

In October 1944 *General* Wittmann assumed command of the elements of the *1. Gebirgs-Division* that had broken out, and with these he established a defensive front in the Drina-Save triangle. After dispersed actions—the Groth group fought in the Kraljevo area in the south, for example—the "First" again went into action as a unit south of Lake Balaton. During the winter, when the front became stationary, the unit was rested and brought up to strength between the Drau and Lake Balaton. This period lasted from 23 November 1944 until 5 March 1945.

Renamed the *1. Volks-Gebirgs-Division*, from 6 to 22 March 1945 the division participated in a battle south of Lake Balaton in Hungary as part of the *LXVIII. Armeekorps* under *General* Konrad, and also the *XXII. Gebirgs-Armeekorps* under *General* Lanz. It was one final defensive success, but the subsequent counterattack became bogged down in the mud.

In the final days of the war the *1. Volks-Gebirgs-Division* under *General* Wittmann fought in the "Reich Protection Position" in the border regions of Burgenland, Styria, and Lower Austria, and then on the eastern flank of the incomplete "Alpine Fortress" south of the Semmering and in the area of Hochwechsel, preventing powerful Soviet forces from breaking into the heart of Austria. During these operations the division fought side by side with the *9. Gebirgs-Division* under *Oberst* Raithel. The army and *Waffen-SS* mountain units made it possible for the *6. Armee* to conduct a somewhat orderly retreat into the "Central Alpine Fortress." After crossing the demarcation line at Hieflau-Liezen the mountain troops were made prisoners of war by the Americans, but were soon released.

While all this was happening, the tragedy of the *LXXXXVII. Armeekorps* under the command of *General* Ludwig Kübler was being played out in the port city of Triest. Among its units was the poorly armed and relatively immobile *188. Gebirgs-Division*. With a rations strength of up to 40,000 men at times, the "Ibex Division" was assigned offensive missions in the "Adriatic Coastland" operations zone. In the final hours it was senselessly sacrificed against a far superior force of regular troops and partisan forces.

On 1 May 1945 the Commander-in-Chief Southeast, *Generaloberst* Löhr, gave Kübler permission to break through with his troops in the direction of the "Alpine Fortress." Despite increasing pressure from his field commanders to take this lifesaving step, Kübler hesitated. Finally, on 6 May 1945, his army corps was forced to surrender to Tito's partisan units. On 6 May 1945 in Graz, Löhr was informed by *Generalfeldmarschall* Kesselring that the *Wehrmacht* was going to surrender on 9 May, and that hostilities would cease at 1000 hours. After desperate attempts to break through near Sembie and Herpelie, countless mountain soldiers were caught in partisan ambushes. Following the infamous "Punishment Marches," the remnants of the *188. Gebirgs-Division* began years of captivity in the hands of the Yugoslavians.

More than 50,000 German and Austrian soldiers, not counting the ethnic Germans in Yugoslavia, lost their lives in Tito's torture chambers and labor camps. Among the victims were the Commander-in-Chief of Army Groups E and Southeast, *Generaloberst* Alexander Löhr, the Commander-in-Chief of Operations Zone Adriatic Coastland and commanding general of the *LXXXXVII. Gebirgs-Armeekorps, General der Gebirgstruppe* Ludwig Kübler, the commander of the *188. Gebirgs-Division, Generalleutnant* Hans von Hößlin, many senior staff officers of the "Ibex Division," and countless commanders and frontline soldiers of the German mountain corps.

Mountain Units in the Balkans

The following senior command organizations and divisions of the German mountain troops were deployed in the Balkans from 1943:

Headquarters, *XV. Gebirgs-Armeekorps* on the Dalmatian Coast and in Croatia;
Headquarters, *XXI. Gebirgs-Armeekorps* in anti-partisan operations in Albania and Montenegro, in the fighting for Sarajevo and in the defensive struggle in Bosnia;
Headquarters, *XXII. Gebirgs-Armeekorps* in Greece and the Ionian islands of Corfu and Cefalonia, in Yugoslavia and in the defensive fighting south of Lake Balaton;
Headquarters, XXXXIX. *Gebirgs-Armeekorps* in the costly fighting in Hungary and Beskides;
the *1. Gebirgs-Division* "in the gorges of the Balkans," where it fought shoulder to shoulder with the *13. Waffen-Gebirgs-Division "Handschar"* of the *Waffen-SS (kroatische Nr. 1)*, but more often with the *7. SS-Freiwilligen-Gebirgs-Division "Prinz Eugen"*;
and the *188. Gebirgs-Division* in the area of Triest, Istria and Fiume.

"Lone vehicles are forbidden to drive this road!" A motorized column in partisan country.

Motorcycle troops of the **1. Gebirgs-Division** *on a well-developed road.*

Generalleutnant Ritter von Stettner observes maneuvers by the 1. Gebirgs-Division in the summer of 1943.

Reconnaissance battalion at rest.

Immediately infantry break camp after a rest stop in the summer heat.

In the gorges of the Balkans.

The leader of a machine-gun team carrying an MG 42 machine-gun with ammunition drum.

Assault team of the **1. Gebirgs-Division** *during maneuvers.*

"Operation Panther," October 1943: heavy field howitzers (Type 18) in firing position.

SS-Obergruppenführer *and* General der Waffen-SS *Artur Phleps, first a highly-decorated officer of the Imperial Austro-Hungarian Army, later commanding general of the Romanian mountain corps, and finally founder of the 7. SS-Freiwilligen-Gebirgs-Division "Prinz Eugen" and commanding general of the V. SS-Gebirgs-Korps, in the front line. Note the Odal rune on the collar patch of the Hauptsturmführer (captain) on the left of the picture. This rune was the symbol of the "Prinz Eugen" Division, whose personnel were largely recruited from the ethnic German population of Transylvania and the Banat.*

226

Motorcyclists of the **7. SS-Freiwilligen-Gebirgs-Division "Prinz Eugen"** *driving through a Bosnian town.*

228

While visiting troops in the Balkans, **Reichsführer-SS** *Heinrich Himmler inspects the equipment and weapons of a* **Waffen-SS** *mountain division. The units of the* **Waffen-SS** *were subordinate to army command in all areas except pay and supply.*

Artur Phleps during a terrain conference. Note his hobnailed mountain boots. Known to his soldiers as "Papa Phleps," he shared tough operational living conditions with his soldiers. Born in Birthälm, Transylvania, in 1881, the general was killed in the fighting there in 1944. Surprised by the advancing Soviets, he was shot immediately after capture.

The Czech-made MG 26(t) light machine-gun could not match the MG 42's rate of fire, but in other respects it was quite good. Many German units were equipped with this weapon, which used a 30-round magazine.

Type 38 H(f) light tank, a captured French vehicle, in operational use by the 7. SS- Gebirgs-Division "Prinz Eugen." The photograph was taken in the Niksic area on 18 May 1943.

The feared 20-mm Vierlingsflak (four-barreled anti-aircraft gun) was equally effective against enemy aircraft and surface targets.

A Czech-made MG 37(t) machine-gun in action against partisans near Presjeka.

Waffen-SS *mountain artillery: heavy artillery in Tomislavgrad firing over the target before commencing the bombardment of enemy mountain positions near Niksic.*

The "Prinz Eugen" Division on the march.

Mountain pioneers of the Waffen-SS *bridging a stream.*

Generaloberst *Dr. Lothar Rendulic visits the* **V. SS-Gebirgs-Korps** *on 31 March 1944. Clearly visible on the uniforms of the* **SS-Obergruppenführer** *and* **General** *der* **Waffen-SS** *Artur Phelps and his aide is the Edelweis emblem of the* **Waffen-SS** *mountain troops, which differed significantly from that of the army's mountain corps.*

On the Croatian Adriatic. Assault boats deliver **Waffen-SS** *mountain infantry to an island occupied by partisans and Badoglio Italians who defected to them.*

Istria Peninsula, spring 1944. Mountain infantry comb the Tolmien-Idria area.

Knight's Cross wearer **Feldwebel** *Johann "Hans" Bauer of the* **6. Kompanie** *of* **Gebirgs-Jäger Regiment** *99 questions a farmer.*

Opposite: **Generalleutnant** *Hans von Hößlin and other officers discuss an upcoming operation against partisans.*

16 April 1944: mountain infantry during "Operation Wendelstein" in the operations zone dubbed "Adriatic Coastland."

Field telephone training against a backdrop of the Julian Alps. Tolmein area, spring 1944.

Mountain artillery during "Operation Wendelstein."

Type 18 light field howitzer (105-mm) in firing position.

241

*The High Savoy, spring 1944. An **Oberjäger** of the mountain troops in front of the Mont Blanc massif, the highest mountain in Europe.*

The War in Italy and the Western Alps 1943-1945

After the end of the fighting in North Africa, in July 1943 Allied forces under Alexander, Montgomery, and Patton successfully invaded Sicily. This brought the Anglo-Americans a swift victory, and Italy to the brink of military and political collapse. After Mussolini was imprisoned, Marshal Badoglio, formerly a loyal fascist, formed a new government. After the Allies landed in southern Italy in September 1943 he decided to reach a separate ceasefire. German troops subsequently disarmed the Italian armed forces. German intelligence discovered that the Duce was being held on the Grans Sasso d'Italia in Abruzzo. Members of an SS commando team under Otto Skorzeny and paratroopers conducted a daring raid to free the Duce. In November 1943 Mussolini founded the *Repubblica Sociale Italiana*. Meanwhile, the provisional government of the Kingdom of Italy, which had gone over to the Allied camp, declared war on Germany.

In heavy and confused fighting, the German Commander-in-Chief in Italy, *Generalfeldmarschall* Albert Kesselring, succeeded in establishing a defensive position on the Volturno (which flows through the southern Apennines between Naples and Rome). The enemy's superiority was tremendous: five times as many infantry, almost 10 times as much artillery and, of course, no shortage of ammunition, fuel, and food. The Allies also enjoyed total control of the skies.

Some of the fiercest fighting took place at Monte Cassino, with its historic Benedictine monastery, founded by the Holy Benedict of Nursia in 525. The *Wehrmacht* intentionally excluded the monastery from its defense lines and also informed the Allies. Based on past experience, however, with the approval of the abbot they evacuated the monastery's unique cultural treasures and priceless library to Rome as a precautionary measure. This measure saved the priceless medieval artifacts from destruction, for what followed surpassed the worst expectations. The Americans and British bombed the monastery until it was a heap of rubble. Quite apart from the moral standpoint, the bombing also proved to be a tactical blunder. The rubble and ruins of the monastery provided a natural defensive position for the German paratroops, mountain troops, and grenadiers. The Allied infantry paid for this miscalculation in blood.

The *5. Gebirgs-Division* took part in the second and third Battles of Monte Cassino after its withdrawal from the Volkhov front (*see* p 132). *Gebirgs-Jäger Regiment 100* saw action at Aquafondata, and *Gebirgs-Jäger Regiment 85* in the peaks of Abruzzo at elevations of up to 2000 meters. There the Germans faced the Free-French troops under General Juin. Although inferior in materiel, the hard-pressed "Fifth" was able to hold its own through skillful use of the terrain. When German troops elsewhere were forced to fall back, there was no longer any point in holding Monte Cassino. Undefeated, the defenders left the mountain and occupied new defensive positions.

The *5. Gebirgs-Division* also withdrew to the north. First, however, *Gebirgs-Jäger Regiment 100* halted an enemy advance in the Norcia area. In mid-July 1944 the regiment reached the Urbino area. When the Battle of Rimini broke out after an American landing there, the mountain troops were once again on the spot to be thrown into the breach. Losses were enormous, however.

In August 1944 the *5. Gebirgs-Division* under *General* Schrank was transferred into the Mont Blanc region. There four battle groups from the division took over the sector between Mont Blanc and Monte Viso. On a front of 260 kilometers, with elevations in excess of 3000 meters, the men of the division guarded the so-called West-Alpine Position. They held strongpoints and positions in the high mountains in spite of severe supply problems. The mountain troops held this mountain front until the end of the war, when they surrendered to the Americans north of Turin.

Before the *5. Gebirgs-Division* arrived in the Western Alps, *General* Pflaum's *157. Reserve-Division* had conducted a costly fighting withdrawal from its former occupation zone in southern France. It pulled back beyond the French-Italian border with a clear mission: to establish positions and defend the mountain passes in the Western Alps, especially at Petit St. Bernhard, with the nearby crossings of Col du Mont and Col de la Seigne, the Mont Cenis and Mont Genévre passes, and at the Col de Larche and the ice regions of the Mont Blanc massif.

On 15 August 1944 the Allies landed in southern France. Caught up in the maelstrom of the fighting retreat was the 157. Reserve-Division, which suddenly had to fight the Allies as well as the partisans. The infantry of the division were called upon to fight partisans at Besançon, Dijon, Chalon, Lyon, Grenoble, and Avignon, and were even sent against the partisan base at Vassieux en Vercors. Clear lines were not reestablished until the retreat to the Alpine passes between France and Italy. It was at this time that the *157. Reserve-Division* was reorganized as the *8. Gebirgs-Division*, equipped and organized to fight in the final high-mountain operations of the Second World War.

Dipl.Ing. Hans Schlemmer, then commanding general of the *LXXV. Armeekorps*, wrote:

"In the difficult small-scale war fought high in the mountains of the Mont Blanc glacier region, the courageous mountain troops fought bravely as in the difficult and costly battles in other theaters."

After its removal from the high-mountain front, the *8. Gebirgs-Division* under *General* Paul Schricker was sent to the Apennines near Bologna, where it faced the American 88th Division, the "Blue Devils." Outnumbered five to one, it fought at Monte Sole, Monte Rumici, and Monte Adone in the Italian mountain range. Shortly before the end of the war the "Kraxler Division" withdrew across the Po into the Alpine Fortress, crossing swords with the American 10th Mountain Division at Lake Garda and in the Etsch Valley. The division received a final honor weeks after the surrender, when a senior American officer came to the POW camp. Speaking on behalf of the commanding officer of the "Blue Devils," he said, "The *8. Gebirgs-Division* and its men fought magnificently."

This assessment applied not just to the *8. Gebirgs-Division*, but to the bulk of the mountain infantry and artillery, pioneers, and members of the mountain signals battalions, pack animal guides, and men of the supply trains; indeed, every mountain soldier who fought honorably in the Second World War according to the rules of war laid down by the Hague and Geneva Conventions.

This photo chronicle is dedicated to them and to every Edelweis soldier who contributed photographs or documents. Its sole purpose is to provide a factual record of the actions of the German mountain troops during the Second World War. I wish to express special thanks to the former chaplain of the *6. Gebirgs-Division*, Prelate Monsignor Johann Georg Schmutz who, shortly before the 70th anniversary of his ordination, gave to me his extensive collection of military-historical records, plus all his diaries, slides, and photographs from his service in France, Greece, and Crete.

Mountain infantryman in the snow-covered Abruzzo.

Machine-gun position in the snow-covered Abruzzo.

Opposite: Mountain infantry officers climbing a mountain some-where in central Italy.

246

Above: A well-earned smoke after a tough march or action.
Facing page: 20-mm light anti-aircraft gun in a mountain position in Abruzzo.

Mountain artillery in firing position at Cassino, 1944.

A field howitzer in action on the Cassino front.

251

The Benedictine monastery of Monte Cassino, completely destroyed by the senseless Allied bombardment.

Spring 1944: morning roll call against the backdrop of Mont Blanc.

Non-commissioned officers of the 157. Division, later the 8. Gebirgs-Division, which served in a defensive role in southern France.

Last roll call in Sallanches.

The trains are loaded and ready to depart from Sallanches. In the foreground are two 75-mm anti-tank guns.

The last anti-tank units guard the transports.

In a village in southern France.

Opposite: Anti-tank gunners training with their 75-mm guns.

Mountain anti-tank gunners hauling their 37-mm anti-tank into position in the French Alps—backbreaking work in the winter snow.

75-mm anti-tank gun in firing position.

50-mm anti-tank guns were also used.

Mountain infantry with dog in the French Western Alps.

Mountain soldier at the foot of the Mont Blanc glacier.

A German mountain soldier and two Italian alpini at the approach to Petit St. Bernhard, autumn 1944.

Mountain strongpoint in the "Western Alps Position."

The Italian-French border, September 1944. Italian auxiliaries build defensive positions for the mountain troops near Villa Nova.

Mont Cenis, April 1945. Two French chasseurs alpines (mountain infantry) are led into captivity. Note the white camouflage covers over their berets.

Position change. The man in the center is carrying a heavy reel of field telephone cable.

Five mountain soldiers in the "Western Alps Position."

The other side: a ski patrol of French mountain infantry.

Final climb—a mountain soldier with his pack animal.

Memorial tablet erected at the former military cemetery of Porta Littoria (La Thuile). It reads: "To our fallen comrades and in memory of all soldiers who died. Erected by members of the 8. Geb.Div. 1952. R.I.P."

Bibliography

The only sources used were division and unit histories, plus relevant biographies and histories of the creation and employment of the German mountain corps in the Second World War.

Alpenkorps in Polen. Im Auftrage des General kommandos XVIII, A.K. Hrsg. von Manz. Innsbruck 1940.

Bauer, Josef Martin: Unternehmen "Elbrus". Das kaukasische Abenteuer 1942. München, Wien 1976.

Bilder aus Lappland. Zu Weihnachten 1942. Hrsg. Oberkommando 20. (Geb,) Armee. Lappland 1942.

Böttger, Gerd: Narvik im Bild. Deutschlands Kampf unter der Mitternachtssonne. Ein Erlebnisbericht in Wort und Bild. 200.-220. Tsd. Oldenburg (Oldb.), Berlin 1943.

Braun, Julius: Enzian und Edelweiß. Die 4. Gebirgsdivision 1940-1945. Bad Nauheim o.J.

Burdick, Charles B.: Hubert Lanz. General der Gebirgstruppe. Osnabrück 1988. (Soldatenschicksale des 20. Jahrhunderts als Geschichtsquelle. Bd. 9.)

Dietl, Gerda-Luise und Herrmann, Kurt (Hrsg,): General Dietl. Bearb. von Max Dingler. Wien 1951.

Fantur, Werner: Narvik. Sieg des Glaubens. Berlin 1941.

Fischer, Hans: Jahre die wir nie vergessen. Das Buch der Gebirgsjäger. München, Wels 1958.

Friedmann, Fr.: Die Sturmfahrt unserer Gebirgsjäger durch Polen. Gefechts- und Erlebnisbericht des 11./ Gebirgs-Jäger-Regiments 100. Berchtesgaden 1939.

Front am Polarkreis. Das Buch eines LapplandKorps. Deutsche Soldaten im finnischen Urwald. Berlin 1943,

Gebirgsjäger erleben Serbien und Ukraine. Hrsg. von Ic der Enzian-Division. München 1942.

Gebirgsjäger in Griechenland und auf Kreta. Hrsg. vom Generalkommando XVIII, (Gebirgs)-Armee-Korps. Bearb. von Tietz und Manz. Berlin 1941.

Gebirgs-Jäger-Regiment 98 im polnischen Feldzug. September 1939. o.0, u. J.

Das Gebirgs-Jäger-Regiment 99 im polnischen Feldzug. Bonn 1939.

Gehring, Egid: Der Stoß in Frankreichs Herz. Der Feldzug einer Gebirgs-Division in Frankreich. Hrsg. im Auftrag des General-Kommandos VII. Armeekorps. München 1941,

Gehring, Egid: Unterm Edelweiß in Jugoslawien. Aus den Erlebnissen einer Gebirgsdivision. Hrsg, im Auftrag des General-Kommandos VII. Armeekorps. München 1941.

Hafner, Ernst: Kampf um Narvik. Heidelberg o.i.

Heß, Wilhelm: Eismeerfront 1941. Aufmarsch und Kampf des Gebirgskorps Norwegen in den Tundren vor Murmansk. Heidelberg 1956. (Die Wehrmacht im Kampf. Bd. 9).

Hölter, Hermann: Armee in der Arktis. Die Operationen der deutschen Lappland-Armee. Bad Nauheim 1953.

Kaltenegger, Roland: Das Deutsche Alpenkorps im Ersten Weltkrieg, Von den Dolomiten nach Verdun, von den Karpaten zum Isonzo, Graz, Stuttgart 1995.

Kaltenegger, Roland: Deutsche Gebirgsjäger im Zweiten Weltkrieg. Stuttgart 1977 (3. Aufl. 1998).

Kaltenegger, Roland-. Die deutsche Gebirgstruppe 1935-1945. München 1989. (2. Neuausgabe 1999).

Kaltenegger, Roland: Edelweiß und Enzian. Die Kriegschronik der 4. Gebirgs-Division 1940-1945. München 2002..

Kaltenegger, Roland: Gebirgsartillerie auf allen Kriegsschauplätzen. Der Kampf der deutschen und österreichischen Gebirgs-Artillerie-Reginnenter im Zweiten Weltkrieg. München 1998.

Kaltenegger, Roland: Gebirgsjäger im Kaukasus. Die Operation "Edelweiß" 1942/43. Graz, Stuttgart 1997

Kaltenegger, Roland. Gebirgssoldaten unter dem Zeichen des "Enzian". Schicksalsweg und Kampf der 4. Gebirgs-Division 1940-1945. Graz, Stuttgart 1983.

Kaltenegger, Roland: Die Gebirgstruppe der Waffen-SS 1941-1945. Wölfersheim-Berstadt 1994. (Nachauflage 1997).

Kaltenegger, Roland: Generaloberst Dietl. Der Held von Narvik. Eine Biographie. München 1990.

Kaltenegger, Roland: Die Geschichte der deutschen Gebirgstruppe 1915 bis heute. Vom Deutschen Alpenkorps des Ersten Weltkrieges zur 1. Gebirgsdivision der Bundeswehr. Stuttgart 1980.

Kaltenegger, Roland: Kampf der Gebirgsjäger um die Westalpen und den Semmering. Die Kriegschroniken der 8. und 9. Gebirgs-Division ("Kampfgruppe Semmering"). Graz, Stuttgart 1987

Kaltenegger, Roland-. Krieg am Eismeer. Gebirgsjäger im Kampf um Narvik, Murmansk und die Murmanbahn. Graz, Stuttgart 1999.

Kaltenegger, Roland. Ludwig Kübler: General der Gebirgstruppe. Stuttgart 1998.

Kaltenegger, Roland: Operation Alpenfestung. Mythos und Wirklichkeit. München 2000.

Kaltenegger, Roland-. Operationszone "Adriatisches Küstenland". Der Kampf um Triest, Istrien und Fiume 1944/45. Graz, Stuttgart 1993. (Sogleich Truppengeschichte der 188. Gebirgs-Division).

Kaltenegger, Roland: Schicksalsweg und Kampf der "Bergschuh"-Division. Die Kriegschronik der 7 Gebirgs-Division, vormals 99. leichte Infanterie-Division, Graz, Stuttgart 1985.

Kaltenegger, Roland: Schörner, Feldmarschall der letzten Stunde. Biographie. München, Berlin 1994 (4. Aufl. 2002).

Kaltenegger, Roland: Die Stammdivision der deutschen Gebirgstruppe. Weg und Kampf der 1. Gebirgs-Division 1935-1945. Graz, Stuttgart 1981.

Kaltenegger, Roland: Waffen und Ausrüstung

der deutschen Gebirgstruppe im Zweiten Weltkrieg. Friedberg/H. (Dornheinn) 1993. (Waffen-Arsenal Sonderband S-31.)

Klatt, Paul: Die 3. Gebirgs-Division 1939-1945. Bad Nauheim 1958.

Konrad, Rudolf: Kampf um den Kaukasus. München o.J.

Kosar, Franz: Gebirgsartillerie. Geschichte, Waffen, Organisation. Stuttgart 1987

Kräutler, Mathias und Springenschmid, Karl: Es war ein Edelweiß. Schicksal und Weg der 2. Gebirgs-Division. Ein Gedenkbuch. 4. Aufl. Graz, Stuttgart 1962.

Kreppel, Hans: Gebirgsartillerie im Kampf. Geschichte des Gebirgs-Artillerie-Regiments 112. 1938-1945. Neugermering b. München 1960.

Lagarde, Jean de-. Deutsche Uniformen 19391945. 2. Aufl. Stuttgart 1999.

Lanz, Hubert: Gebirgsjäger. Die 1. Gebirgsdivision 1935-1945. Bad Nauheim 1954.

Lanz, Hubert: Gebirgs-Jäger-Reginnent 100 - Kurzgeschichte. München o.J.

Manz: Wir vom Alpenkorps. Erinnerungsbuch für die Soldaten des XVIII. A.K. Im Auftrage des Generalkommandos XVIII. A.K. zusammengestellt u. hrsg. 3. Aufl. Innsbruck 1939.

Marek, Kurt VV.: Wir hielten Narvik. Berlin 1942.

Nerbuch, Volker: Parole Lemberg. Die Sturmfahrt der 1. Gebirgsdivision im Polenfeldzug 1939. München o.J.

Pichlsberger, Franz-. Deutsche Gebirgsjäger an der Eismeerfront. Berlin, Leipzig 1943.

Rabensteiner, Wolf: Der Soldat im Gebirge. Salzburg 1961.

Ringel, Julius: Hurra, die Ganns! Ein Gedenkbuch für die Soldaten der 5. Gebirgs-Division. Bearb. von Fritz Weber. 8. Aufl. Graz, Stuttgart o.J.

Rüf, Hans: Gebirgsjäger vor Murmansk. Der Kampf des Gebirgskorps "Norwegen" an der Eis meerfront 1941/42. Innsbruck 1957

Ruef, Karl: Gebirgsjäger zwischen Kreta und Murmansk. Die Schicksale der 6. Gebirgs- Division. 3. Aufl. Graz, Stuttgart o.J.

Ruef, Karl: Odyssee einer Gebirgsdivision. Die 3. Gebirgs-Division im Einsatz. Graz, Stuttgart 1976.

Ruef, Karl: Winterschlacht im Mai. Die Zerreißprobe des Gebirgskorps Norwegen (XIX. Geb. A.K.) vor Murmansk. Graz, Stuttgart 1984.

Ruppert, A.: Front am Polarkreis. Das Buch eines Lappland-Korps. Berlin 1943.

Schlicht, Adolf und Angolia, John R.: Die deutsche Wehrmacht. Uniformierung und Ausrüstung